GREAT STAGECOACH
ROBBERIES
OF THE
OLD WEST

GREAT STAGECOACH ROBBERIES
OF THE
OLD WEST

R. MICHAEL WILSON

TWODOT®

GUILFORD, CONNECTICUT
HELENA, MONTANA
AN IMPRINT OF THE GLOBE PEQUOT PRESS

A · TWODOT® · BOOK

Copyright © 2007 by R. Michael Wilson

Text design by Lisa Reneson
Map by Melissa Baker © Morris Book Publishing, LLC
Spot art throughout © Clipart.com

Library of Congress Cataloging-in-Publication Data
Wilson, R. Michael, 1944-
   Great stagecoach robberies of the Old West / R. Michael Wilson.
   — 1st ed.
     p. cm.
   Includes bibliographical references and index.
   ISBN-13: 978-0-7627-4127-4
   ISBN-10: 0-7627-4127-9
   1. Stagecoach robberies—West (U.S.)—History. 2. Brigands and
robbers—West (U.S.)—History. 3. Outlaws—West (U.S.)—History.
I. Title.
HV6661.W47W55 2007
364.15'52097809034—dc22

                                                    2006018314

Manufactured in the United States of America
First Edition/First Printing

CONTENTS

ACKNOWLEDGMENTS

No historical work of detail and accuracy can be written without the extensive support of many organizations and experts. *Great Stagecoach Robberies of the Old West* is no exception, and following is a list of those who made this book possible:

Albertson's Library, Boise (Idaho) State University; American Medical Association; Arizona State Historical Society; Arizona Territorial Prison Historic State Park; Bancroft Library at Berkeley, California; California State Historical Society; Denver Public Library; Doug Engebretson, author; Walter I. Faber, firearms and equestrian expert; Paul J. Higbee, Spearfish, South Dakota, historian; Idaho State Historical Society; Montana State Historical Society; National Archives and Record Administration; Nevada County (California) Historical Society; Nevada Historical Society; Nevada State Archives; New Hampshire State Historical Society; Oregon State Historical Society; Pinal County (Arizona) Historical Society; Sharlot Hall Museum Archive; South Dakota State Historical Society; South Dakota Department of Tourism and State Development; Larry Walker of Magazine House; Wells, Fargo & Company Museum; Britt Wilson, author; Wyoming State Archives.

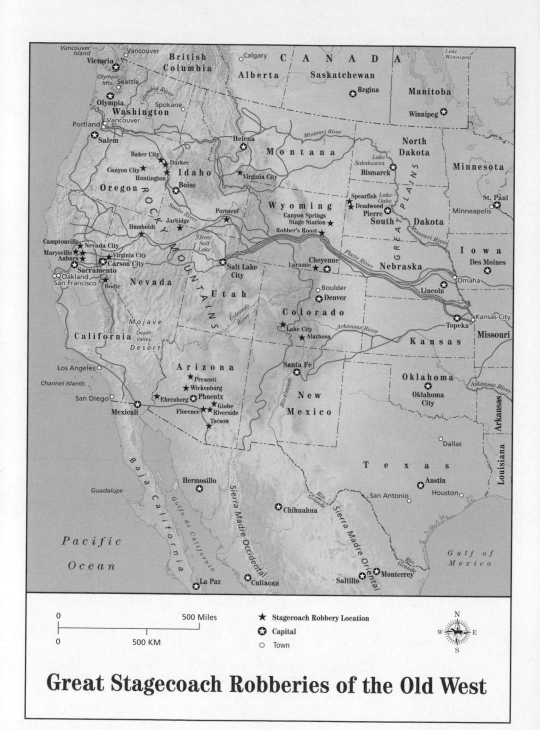

Great Stagecoach Robberies of the Old West

INTRODUCTION

The first "Old West" stagecoach attacked and robbed was traveling to Marysville, California, in 1856, seven years after gold was discovered at Sutter's Mill. Six decades later, in December 1916, the last stagecoach robbery was accomplished at Jarbidge, Nevada. During those sixty years stagecoaches were attacked in sixteen of the seventeen western states, with North Dakota the only state spared the experience. Many of the hundreds of western stagecoach robberies were failed attempts and many more were "water hauls," where nothing or plunder of very little value was aboard. Only when the loot was substantial, or someone was badly wounded or killed, was there a sufficient reward offered for the capture of the road agents. Without a reward there was little motivation to pursue road agents because it was government policy to withhold reimbursement for expenses unless the pursuit resulted in an arrest and conviction. From the small number of "successful" stagecoach robberies only a very few rise to a level of greatness.

The circumstances that would foster the emergence of the road agent began to develop in 1849 as soon as gold was discovered at Sutter's Mill, and the rush was on. Men from around the world flooded onto the Pacific coast in search of riches. Mining, it turned out, was a lonely business and homesick miners could hardly wait for some word from home to distract them from their daily routine.

Alexander Todd joined in the search for gold about November 1, 1849, but soon learned that few men struck it rich for all the work and time they put in. By December Todd saw what the camps needed. He appeared in Jacksonville, not far from the gold diggings, and offered to bring in the mails, which were then piled high at the post office in San Francisco awaiting delivery. Todd left with a packet of signed letters of authorization and soon returned with sacks of mail. The miners were pleased with this young entrepreneur and felt they could trust him, so they asked him to carry their gold dust to San Francisco and deposit it in one of the new banks established there for that purpose. He agreed to do the job and took his first load of dust, estimated at about $200,000 or just less than 15,000 ounces, down the San Joaquin River and across San Francisco Bay in a rowboat. In San Francisco Todd used his share to out- fit a pack train and returned to the camps with the miner's receipts and mail.

A pack train was the only alternative to the dangerous water route, as there were no roads, and in some places the trails were almost too rough and rugged for mules or men. While this seemed the perfect scenario for a road agent to operate, there were no robberies in those early days and Todd later explained:

An express man on the road was almost exempt from interference because everybody was interested, and if an express man had been attacked, and his assailant discovered, punishment would have been very speedy . . . An express man though carrying large sums of money, bore almost a charmed life in those days.

Before 1849 express companies were active throughout the East and Midwest, but there was only one small operation on the Pacific Coast. The Adams Express Company soon established itself as the major provider of express shipping in California. By 1854 Adams had grown to dominate the entire Pacific coast, while the men behind Wells, Fargo & Company carefully watched the developing situation.

Finally in 1852, Wells, Fargo opened its Pacific-coast business and posted its first public notice in the *New York Times* on May 20:

WELLS, FARGO & CO. CALIFORNIA EXPRESS

Capital $300,000

A joint stock company.   Office 16 Wall Street

This company having completed its organization as above is now ready to undertake the general forwarding agency and commission business; the purchase and sale of gold dust, bullion and specie, also packages, parcels and freight of all description in and between the City of New York and the City of San Francisco, and the principal cities and towns in California.

A similar notice appeared in San Francisco's *Alta California* in early June 1852, before the company had opened its first office and even before its representatives arrived on the Pacific Coast. Once established, the company grew quickly by adopting a policy of acquiring its smaller competitors, which had appeared during the previous three years. As early as November 1852, Wells, Fargo & Company bought Gregory and Company's Express; in September 1853 it acquired Reynolds, Todd and Company Express; in July 1854 it added Hunter and Company's Express. That left Wells, Fargo & Company with only one important competitor in the West—the Adams Express Company.

The Adams Express Company concentrated on its waning express business in association with Page, Bacon and Company, a banking firm that was located in the same building in San Francisco. The parent bank of Page, Bacon was located in St. Louis and had invested heavily in the Ohio and Mississippi Railroad. When that venture failed, the parent bank was forced to close its doors. The San Francisco branch had just sent $1 million in assets to the parent bank, and, when word of the St. Louis closure reached San Francisco on February 23, 1855, the local branch was unable to meet the demand and also had to close its doors. Adams and Company at San Francisco followed suit, never to reopen in California.

In June 1849 the first stage line in California, the Maurison & Company Express and Mail Line from Stockton to the Stanislaus Mines, was established when it advertised in the *Alta California*. The "coaches" were spring or dead-axle wagons pulled by teams of two or four mules or horses, as there were no true coaches in California until the first coach arrived by ship on June 24, 1850. The next shipment of Concord stagecoaches arrived by ship in 1851 and the first Butterfield Overland coach would not arrive from St. Louis until October 7, 1858. In those early days there were few roads that could accommodate any form of stagecoach, but this changed slowly over the first five years. Finally roads were established, though they were often little more than a worn track of wagon wheels. Stagecoaches began to replace pack trains and freight wagons.

When gold and silver were discovered in Nevada, Wells, Fargo, now the dominant express company in the West, added stage lines to its operations. It purchased the Pioneer Stage Line in 1864 and on November 1, 1866, added the entire Holladay Overland Mail & Express Company. In 1869 Wells, Fargo & Company sold its stage lines and thereafter contracted the handling of express in its "green treasure boxes" on whichever stage lines operated regionally.

After the little green treasure box became the standard for carrying express, other companies included making up boxes as part of the process of "stocking the road." The treasure boxes used by Wells, Fargo & Company were manufactured by J. Y. Ayer of San Francisco. Ayer used ponderosa pine for the body, which he reinforced with oak rims and iron strapping. A Wells, Fargo & Company box measured 20 inches long by 12 inches high by 10 inches deep and weighed nearly twenty-five pounds

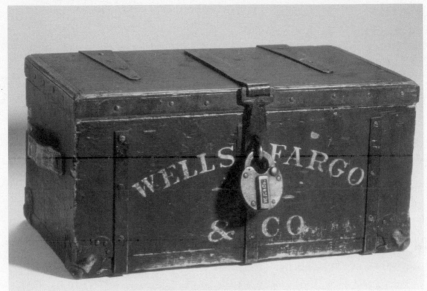

Wells Fargo treasure box
WELLS FARGO BANK, N.A.

"lean." At first these boxes were loaded in the office and deposited into the driver's boot or inside the passenger compartment, but the common command of "throw down that box" led to its being bolted into the boot or body in later years.

The earliest stage line to cross the southwestern desert was James E. Birch's line from San Antonio, Texas, to San Diego, California, in 1857. In 1858 John Butterfield's Overland Mail Company took over most of that route and the mail contract and extended the line to San Francisco. But, with the opening of hostilities between the states, the line was moved north, and the Overland line, which had been surprisingly efficient, was rarely on schedule during that period.

Besides the transcontinental stagecoach line, there were innumerable independent stage lines in operation in every region, but these often did not do well. In Arizona, for example, the firm of Caldwell and Levalley ran a line between Phoenix and Prescott in anticipation of winning the mail contract when it came up for bid but were disappointed when their competitor, Kerens & Mitchell, underbid them. They had to reduce their semiweekly to a weekly service and then on one trip refused to take a shipment of gold bullion saying their coach was disabled and would be repaired at Prescott. However, when they got to their station on the Agua Fria River they put Levalley's family aboard and had a Mexican employee drive their stock along as they "skipped the country" toward New Mexico via the Little Colorado River. A constable went in pursuit with an attachment for their property but not a warrant for their arrest. He overtook them and, when they made good on the debts listed, he allowed them to continue east.

When the term "stagecoach" is uttered, one is reminded of a beautifully decorated Concord coach rocking along behind six powerful, perfectly matched horses. Passengers are envisioned reclining in the roomy interior while the roof and rear boot is laden with their luggage, goods, and express booked for the next destination. Concord coaches, which were built by the Abbott and Downing Company in Concord, Massachusetts, measured 8½ feet long and high and 5 feet wide, and weighed 2,500 pounds. The body was egg shaped and rested on thick leather through-braces running front to back, which let the body rock and earned it many nicknames including "Pitching Betsy." The Concord coach in the 1840s cost $1,200 to $1,500, and the price rose only slowly over the next several decades. A Concord coach could carry twenty-one people, nine inside and twelve on top, including the driver and messenger.

However it was not the shape or size of a vehicle that determined if it was a "stagecoach," but its use. A stagecoach was any four-wheeled vehicle pulled by horses or mules that was used as a public conveyance but also carried the U.S. mails, and few stage lines could survive without a mail contract. A lucrative contract to carry express, such as a contract with Wells, Fargo & Company, made the stage line profitable. The fares from passengers made it a success. While a coach might not be carrying mail, express, and passengers on every run, it must have been able to do so in order to be a "stagecoach."

By 1856, the year of the first stagecoach robbery, there were hundreds of stagecoaches in operation on the West Coast. As the stagecoach business matured, many Concord-like wagons were built at western carriage works. However, on many routes all that was needed for a particular run was a celerity or "mud" wagon, a dead-axle or spring wagon such as a buckboard, or a surplus army ambulance. These conveyances, and sometimes the Concords, lumbered along behind teams of horses or mules often mismatched in size and appearance. Teams consisted of two, four, or six animals, depending on the vehicle, weather, and terrain. Often the stock was so poor that Prescott, Arizona's *Daily Miner* newspaper referred to them as "skeletons covered with horsehide, which the company fondly hoped would make this trip before dying . . . "

Passengers were allowed twenty-five pounds of luggage, two blankets, one canteen, a duster coat, hat, and clothing. They were given a cramped space in which to sit, often sharing the interior with mail sacks or express packages and the express box or safe bolted to the floor of the interior. The rocking and rolling of the coach could cause passengers to become queasy, and they would be subjected to all sorts of insects, choking dust, and little sleep.

There were worse times for some passengers, however, as a stagecoach might be delayed at some remote station for days due to swollen rivers, or a coach might be mired in mud, requiring the passengers to disembark and pull it and the horses out. Temperatures could be unbearably hot or, as stage-line entrepreneur James O. Grant noted while crossing the Arizona desert in 1870, "It was so cold that it almost froze the driver and passengers." A coach might also careen out of control and roll over or drop off a steep edge, or some mishap might lead to the loss of the team and perhaps even the driver, as in the following instance:

The wheelers fell and while the driver was extricating them, the leaders broke away and ran off. The driver was so frightened that he concluded to throw up his job and then and there struck out for newer pastures, and we understand he has not since been heard of. His only passengers, two ladies, were considerably frightened. The hostler went out from the station and brought the team in.

"Stage" in stagecoach referred to the division of a route into segments or "stages" of travel—15 to 20 miles between stations under ideal circumstances—though over time the term "stage" was commonly applied to the coach. Swing stations were quite basic, with corrals, a shed to store feed, and living quarters for a hostler. At a swing station the teams were changed in less than fifteen minutes, depending upon whether the animals were in the corral or out to pasture, and passengers barely had time to make their toilet. Swing stations alternated with way stations, and at these larger facilities passengers could eat a meal, though the stop was often for less than a half hour. Sometimes when a stagecoach stopped for the night, a way station would allow passengers to sleep in the large front room, which also served as the dining room, bar, and sometimes a store.

After a day's travel on a through-coach, the driver and the coach might also be exchanged before continuing on. In the desert the distances between stations could be considerably longer, as these stations were at first situated only where water was available. If the distance was too great between stations, then a dry station would be established and water would be hauled to a tank built by the company. In the earliest time, before dry stations could be supplied, remudas of horses or mules were driven along with the coach for periodic changes of the team. Later, as these routes became better established, wells were dug at regular intervals and, once water was found, stations were built at those sites.

One of the greatest hazards, or at least the most thrilling event, during travel on a stagecoach was being stopped and robbed by a road agent. Before a road agent appeared in a region, there would have to be something of great value to be stolen, something worth the hardships, the effort, and the risk. Treasure most often took the form of a precious metal, such as gold or silver, coming from the mines, but either of these in the form of coins along with greenbacks could be carried as a payroll going to the mines. Both the up and down coaches were in jeopardy of being robbed.

The discovery of rich ore created the "boom" town from which the treasure would be shipped. Boom towns literally sprang up overnight wherever rich ore was discovered, and these temporary towns of tents and makeshift buildings often grew to thousands of souls within weeks. Some boomtowns eventually became permanent; others ghost towns. Boomtowns would have a stamp mill built to refine the ore. The results of that refining process would be shipped to another destination in the form of bullion or dust to be forwarded to a bank, and the destination was usually a previously established town or a railroad depot. Road agents would not be interested in tons of raw ore, but bullion or dust was better than paper currency.

As soon as a boomtown was set up, it was immediately necessary to build a road to the new site so that equipment, supplies, building materials, and miners could be taken to the mines and the heavy bullion taken out. These roads could be built by a variety of means. In Nevada some roads were built by franchise, whereby the builder would recover his expenses by collecting a toll from those who used his portion of the road. In another instance a Nevada man built his own road just so he could establish a stage line. In Arizona there were, in places, roads formed over the centuries by the natural flow of the desert's rare rainstorms. Sometimes private citizens might subscribe a sum for a man to undertake the building or improvement of a road. Some roads were built inadvertently, as in Oregon where large teams of mules pulled heavy sleds laden with huge mining machinery over rough trails, grading them as they moved along. Once a road was built, a stage line could be established. This required the positioning of a series of stations that had to be stocked with everything the coach might need including horses or mules for a change of team, feed, harnesses, king pins, wheels, grease, and all the other necessities to keep the wagons rolling.

After the stage line was established, the road agent could make his appearance. He would make a careful survey of the route and select an isolated location that would provide him time to make his escape. This site would be a place where the coach would be traveling at a rate of speed slower than the usual 8 to 9 miles per hour, such as a steep ascending grade where the horses would be tired and stop to "blow" at the brow, in the soft sand of the desert, or at a sharp curve in the road. Where a proper site did not present itself, the road agent could create one by building an obstruction or by just tying a rope across the road. A road agent operated on foot, as the back of a horse provided an unstable platform from which to conduct his business, and any sudden sound such as the report of a gunshot could cause a horse to bolt and throw its rider. The road agent would surprise the slow-moving coach from behind a tree or from the brush along side the road and, with gun drawn, make his demands. Sometimes the suddenness of a road agent's appearance or the firing of a shot frightened the stage horses, or the driver whipped up his team at the first sign of danger, and the coach was carried to safety.

The intelligence regarding the treasure aboard a coach was often faulty or the robber simply gambled in selecting the time to make his move and missed his loot. All too often the robber found nothing aboard, such as the time the treasure box contained only a 25-cent bottle of patent medicine, or another incident when two robbers had to settle for an orange apiece to quench their thirst.

The amount of treasure taken often determined the effort that would be expended in pursuing road agents, especially during the early days when there were no funds allocated to pursue stagecoach robbers. Lawmen had to rely upon rewards for the capture and conviction of road agents, or depend upon the reward for recovered treasure, to reimburse them for their expenses. When nothing of value was taken and no one was injured or killed, there was no reward, and little or no effort was made to make an arrest. Robbing the U.S. mails, a federal offense, was an exception; some robbers learned to leave the mails unmolested. In response the postal department determined that merely delaying the U.S. mails would be considered a federal offense, and in that way it could keep the U.S. marshal on the case.

As railroads began to appear across the country, stage-line owners expressed great concern. Stagecoaching men thought that the completion of a railroad in their area of operation would spell an end to their stagecoach line, but the railroads brought in new population and new businesses. The stage-line owners found, to their surprise, that their businesses flourished. Many new routes and lines were added to bring passengers, express, and mail to the railroads and to take the same away to every town and settlement. Railroads did finally spell an end to "stages" as more lines operated over shorter distances, often point to point and back without any station stops in between, but it was the automobile that finally wrought the end of "coaches" as a means of public transportation. Stagecoaches were operating in some areas until well into the twentieth century and an Arizona stage line was still delivering the U.S. mail until the dirt road to the town of Young was paved and the coach was replaced by a Ford in 1928.

There were hundreds of stagecoaches "jumped" before the last robbery occurred in December 1916, but the majority of these were relatively uneventful experiences, except for the passengers and driver. Only a small fraction of these heinous offences rise to a level of greatness, and those that follow are among the most thrilling milestones of stagecoach robbery in the Old West.

CHAPTER ONE

THE FIRST STAGECOACH ROBBERY IN THE WEST

Thomas J. Hodges, hideously disfigured and well educated in crime at California's newly built San Quentin prison, adopted Tom Bell as his criminal alias. He had been a barroom brawler in his earlier days and in one affray had his nose crushed so badly that it was nearly flat against his face, except for the small protrusion that had a deep dent in the tip. This repulsive twenty-six-year-old man escaped prison with several other convicts, and formed a gang that embarked upon a rampage of petty, sometimes laughable, crimes throughout central California. He would have joined other petty criminals in obscurity had he not been a devious and ingenious gang leader. Hodges devised a plan to stop and rob a stagecoach in transit, something no one else had dared try. But happenstance intervened and three of his six road agents were drawn off by an unexpected rider, leaving an opportunity for the stagecoach to escape. The situation turned tragic when a stray bullet killed an innocent female passenger. More deaths would follow.

The early record of Tom Bell is confusing because under his real name of Hodges, he had at some time, adopted the sobriquet "Doc" or "Doctor," so it had been assumed for a century and a half that he had graduated from some medical school before his seventeenth birthday. To add to the confusion, it had been reported all those years that, upon graduating from medical school in 1847, Hodges enlisted in the Tennessee Volunteers under Colonel Frank Cheatham. Reportedly he served as a "medical attaché" in the war with Mexico, having been refused officer status because of his young age. What the record actually reveals is that Hodges never graduated from medical school and probably never attended one. He never enlisted in the Tennessee Volunteers and did not serve during the Mexican War. The position of medical attaché did not even exist, as medical staff designations were doctor, nurse, or hospital steward.

What is known of Hodges is that soon after gold was discovered in California, he drifted toward the goldfields, arriving in 1850 to search for his fortune. He failed to make a strike and soon turned to petty crime to survive. When this proved successful, he embarked on more serious criminal endeavors to increase his plunder.

Hodges was arrested in 1851 for breaking into a cabin and ransacking the contents and, to protect his respectable family in Rome, Tennessee, adopted an alias from an Auburn thief of small renown— Tom Bell. This was the only name he would use thereafter, which he was certain would confuse lawmen when he returned to his criminal career.

In 1851 Tom Bell was convicted and sentenced to a term on the *Waban,* a 268-ton prison bark anchored at Angel Island in San Francisco Bay across from Point San Quentin. The convicts, whether sentenced to hard labor or not, were employed quarrying stone for the new prison being built across the bay. Bell had not been in prison long when he managed to escape by feigning illness but was soon captured and returned to complete his sentence. In late 1854 he escaped again, this time with six men whom he would later enlist into his gang. One of these men, serving time as Bill White though his real name was Bill Gristy, would become his first lieutenant and close friend. However, White would eventually betray Bell.

Bell enlisted Ned Convery, alias Connor, and Jim Smith both of whom had escaped prison with him. He added to their rolls Montague

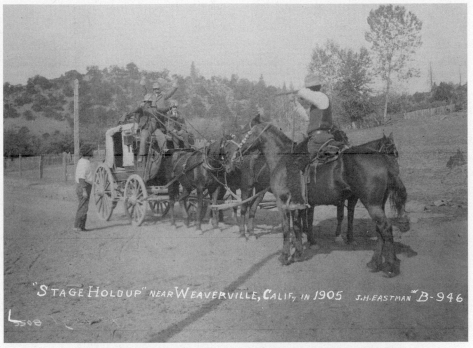

"STAGE HOLDUP" NEAR WEAVERVILLE, CALIF, IN 1905   J.H. EASTMAN "B-946

Reenactment of a stage holdup near Weaverville, California
J.H. EASTMAN COLLECTION, B-946, SPECIAL COLLECTIONS,
UNIVERSITY OF CALIFORNIA LIBRARY, DAVIS

Lyon, known as "Monte Jack," who brought with him Juan Rocher, alias
Juan Fernandez. "English" Bob Carr also joined the ranks, and these
seven men formed the nucleus of Bell's gang. Because they would enlist
many others from time to time, Bell, in typical youthful exuberance,
devised a secret method of identification for his transient corps—a bullet with a hole drilled through and tied to a string, which the gang member would dangle in plain view when he wanted to be identified by
someone.

Bell established three headquarters: the Mountaineer House,
operated by Jack Phillips, on the Folsom to Auburn road; the California
House on the Camptonville Road near Marysville; and on the road
between Sacramento and Nevada City, the Western Exchange Hotel,
which was operated by Mrs. Elizabeth Hood. After the operators at these

three popular hostels provided Bell with intelligence on which travelers were carrying substantial funds, he divided his men into teams and sent them out to gather in the loot.

Bell's plan was to have his men always make it known that the victims were being robbed by Tom Bell, so it seemed possible for Bell to strike one place in the morning and then appear 200 miles away that evening. His plan was to confuse lawmen so that he could easily escape capture or prove an alibi if arrested, and that worked for some time. Bell was 6 feet 1 inch in height, quite tall for those times; he had broad shoulders but was gaunt in appearance; he had blond hair, which he wore to his shoulders; and he had a sandy moustache, which he trimmed so it connected with his sandy goatee. While this description could have fit many men in old California, Bell's crushed nose was quite distinctive. This characteristic made it possible for the lawmen, once they began sharing intelligence, to determine when the real Tom Bell was involved. Bell, it was learned, had two fine horses he used regularly— one named Buckskin because of his color and the other a fine-blooded mare. Identifying Tom Bell's horse aided greatly in identifying the guilty culprit.

Bell's gang robbed a vegetable peddler and a lager deliveryman in the spring of 1856 and were active in a variety of petty crimes during the early summer months of 1856. This led Bell to conclude that they should try something more substantial. Bell ordered his men to lie low through-out the latter days of summer while he made plans. He decided it was time to try something entirely new to the criminal element of California—stopping a moving stagecoach filled with armed passengers. Even before Bell's plan stagecoaches were not exempt from crime. Luggage was often pilfered and the front and rear boots rifled for plunder while the vehicle was stopped at depots or stage stations. What Bell planned was not entirely innovative either. Dick Turpin (1706–1739) had stopped and robbed coaches in England a century earlier, and stage-coach robbers would be known as Turpins until two highwaymen stopped at a stage station and reported that they were "agents of the road." When this was relayed, Wells, Fargo & Company afterwards referred to highwaymen as "road agents."

◇ ◇ ◇

On the morning of August 12, 1856, Sam Langston's Express Company stagecoach pulled out of Camptonville for Marysville with John Greer (sometimes spelled Gear) driving and Bill Dobson riding as shotgun messenger. Between Dobson's legs rested the treasure box containing $100,000 in gold dust. A gold-dust dealer from Camptonville named Rideout, the major contributor to the treasure in the box, had elected to ride his horse ahead of the stagecoach to avoid the dust kicked up by the coach's wheels and horses. He declined to ride in the coach because he suffered motion sickness when rocking to and fro in a "pitching Betsy."

The stagecoach stopped at the California House 25 miles from Marysville. Here Smith Sutton, disguised as a miner, got off. He was Bell's chief spy in Camptonville and confirmed that the treasure was aboard.

The stage pulled out at 1:00 P.M. with Rideout still in the lead. Bell mounted, rode down a wash to collect his men, and then rode hard to get ahead of the stagecoach. Just before 4:30 P.M. Rideout came to the fork in the road to Marysville, only minutes ahead of the coach and decided to take the alternate, slightly longer high road where many large trees offered shade on that warm afternoon. The fork was only a few miles from town, and the trip would soon come to an end without any unto-ward event; Rideout relaxed in his saddle. However, the gold-dust dealer had not ridden more than 100 yards when "Monte Jack," "English" Bob Carr, and Juan Rocher rode out of the brush and covered him with their six-shooters. They ordered him to dismount and took his horse. He started toward the ravine, intending to climb down to the stage road and hitch a ride on the coach, when the men called him back and went through his empty pockets, then ordered him down to the road where he intended going anyway. The three men sat on their mounts, one holding

17

the reins of Rideout's horse, and watched their victim struggle through the heavy brush.

As soon as Rideout got to the stage road, he heard the coach coming and was about to wave at the driver to stop when Tom Bell, Bill Gristy, and Ned Convery rode out of the brush on the other side of the road and covered Greer and Dobson with revolvers. Bell ordered the coach to halt. Meanwhile, the three men who had taken Rideout's horse were riding as hard as they could through the heavy brush of the ravine, as they were supposed to have been on the opposite side of the coach covering the two stage men. Their absence proved to be the plan's undoing. Dobson could have made no move if he'd been covered from two sides, but with all three targets on one side of the coach, he did not hesitate and opened fire with his rifle.

Several armed passengers joined in the fracas with their revolvers. Convery was wounded slightly and unhorsed, so the other two men retreated into the brush pulling their wounded companion with them. The stage proceeded on at a run as the three horse thieves arrived on the scene and fired after the coach. In their haste to try a second time to stop the stagecoach, they dropped the reins to Rideout's horse, and he swung into the saddle and raced after the coach. Dobson, though wounded in his arm, swung around as the three newcomers fired after the fleeing coach, and shot Rocher out of his saddle—or at least the horse bolted and threw its rider. In all over forty shots were exchanged in less than a minute, but not one of the robbers was seriously wounded.

When Rideout caught up with the coach, Greer told him to ride ahead and sound the alarm. The driver said they would take stock of the situation when they were safe in Marysville. The town was quickly alerted, so everyone was on the street when the coach arrived. The passengers had already determined that in addition to Dobson's arm wound, John Campbell had received a grazing shot to his forehead and another man had been shot in both legs. Worst of all the black wife of the town barber, Mrs. Tilghman, had been shot through the brain and died instantly. In addition, the crowd learned that a white male passenger and four

Chinese male passengers had fled from the coach when it was attacked and were probably still stumbling through the brush on the outskirts of town. As the robbers had not thought to wear masks, it was clear from the description that it was the Bell gang, led by Bell himself.

Robbery was one thing, murder another. Throughout Northern California citizens demanded that the Bell gang be rounded up and hanged or imprisoned. In Sacramento Detectives Robert Harrison and Daniel Gay were assigned to capture and destroy the Bell gang, and they were not to undertake any other tasks until they succeeded. Captain Bill King of the Marysville police swore in a posse and started on the robbers' trail. King was so persistent that Bell wrote him a letter in which he tried to trade information on other crimes and criminals and offered a monetary bribe. He challenged the lawman, "Catch me if you can," but also suggested that he would consider an armistice, but King refused to reply to the offer.

In September Detective Harrison and his new partner, J. M. Anderson of Marysville, captured a member of the Bell gang named Tom Brown. Brown could not tell them anything about Bell but did disclose where five members of the gang were camped. The detectives made their plans and enlisted the help of Captain A. J. Barclay and an unnamed butcher known for being a crack shot. They went to the camp near the Mountaineer House, arriving at night. The plan was for the prisoner to go ahead of the two detectives, open the flap, and then greet the men inside. The detectives then would jump in and cover the fugitives with their double-barreled shotguns. The other two posse men would remain outside and keep a bead on the tent with rifles and, if there was any shooting, riddle the tent with bullets.

All went well until George Walker grabbed a pistol from the table when told to surrender and replied, "No, never!" He was killed instantly with a load of buckshot in his chest. The detectives, knowing that the tent would be shot to pieces in seconds, fell to the floor. This gave Bill Gristy the chance to escape under the side of the tent. He got away though he suffered a severe wound to his scalp. Outlaw Nicanora

Rodriguez tried to follow but was shot in the hip. Meanwhile Anderson covered Brown, Adolph Newton, and a Mexican, known only as Domingo, with his shotgun still fully loaded in both barrels, preventing a further breakout. The posse, though disappointed with Gristy's escape, took Brown, Newton, Rodriguez, and Domingo to jail and brought in the dead body of Walker, declaring it a good night's work.

Meanwhile "Monte Jack" had been hiding at the ranch of a man named Ramirez. When a posse went there to capture him, the Mexican resisted and was shot dead, allowing Monte Jack to escape. Two days later word came that a number of gang members were in custody at the Oregon House. When the posse arrived there and sorted through the prisoners, three more of Bell's gang were jailed, but no one of importance. During the following days, five more of Bell's men were captured and jailed by Captain William P. Calloway of Marysville. Jack Phillips of the Mountaineer House was arrested for harboring fugitives and providing Bell's men with intelligence on potential victims.

Placer County Sheriff William T. Henson was the next to encounter gang members and nearly capture Bell. He got word that some of the gang was at the Franklin House near Auburn. When he arrived with his posse, he found Bell, Ned Convery, and Perry "Texas" Owens mounted. A gunfight followed in which Convery was killed, but Bell and Owens got away. The two fugitives knew they had to hide for a few weeks until winter set in, when the cold and heavy rains might discourage the posses searching for them. Bell established a base camp and sent out word to Bill Gristy to join him. He also sent for Elizabeth Hood and her three daughters to come and keep house. He hired two brothers named Farnsworth, too old to be gang members, to chop wood, to tend the animals, and to do the other chores necessary for the upkeep of a frontier farm.

Gristy had been active robbing travelers with a Mexican partner, so when he got word to join Bell, he started out bringing along the Mexican. When the pair got as far as Knight's Ferry, not far from Firebaugh's Ferry, they decided to go into the sleepy little farming community and have a good meal. They were in an area of California where the Bell gang had never operated and were sure they would not be recognized, but they had not sat down to dinner before they were arrested. It was a remarkable coincidence that Major T. W. Lane, a close friend of the Angel Island Prison warden, was in town. He had visited the prison two years earlier and recognized Gristy as Bill White, before he had escaped from that institution, and knew him to be a member of the Bell gang. After a night in the stone jailhouse, Gristy and the Mexican were ready to negotiate. After Gristy told all about Bell's hideout, he was sent north to stand trial while the Mexican was held as a guide.

Lane and Sheriff D. L. Mulford each formed a posse and started for a farm 6 miles above Firebaugh's Ferry. When they arrived, they found that a posse had been camped there for a day, and Bell had not appeared. They camped for a week, but when no other gang members showed by Saturday, October 4, they broke camp and started for their respective homes. Sheriff Mulford's posse left for Stockton in San Joaquin County, and Major Lane's posse for Knight's Ferry.

Robert Price, a member of Lane's posse, started for his home in Sonora by another route and, upon crossing the river to take the road northeast, saw a man hiding in the brush. His suspicious actions alerted Price, and he turned his horse and headed after the Lane posse. They returned to the location at 11:00 A.M. and found a tall, slender man relaxing in his saddle while talking with a mounted Mexican. They got the drop on him and asked his name, an unnecessary question when they saw his distinct features.

Judge George D. Belt, a member of the posse, said, "I believe that you are the man we have been looking for." Bell replied, "very probably." They tied their prisoner's hands and took him to Firebaugh's Ferry, arriving at 4:00 P.M. Lane then sent a man after Sheriff Mulford.

At the ferry Bell admitted his identity. The men discussed the events leading up to his capture, and Bell asked for the opportunity to tell all before they hanged him. The men talked it over and refused his offer. But when Bell asked for time to write to Mrs. Hood and to his mother, paper, pen, and ink were provided.

The men, now concerned that Sheriff Mulford might arrive and demand custody, discussed their next move and went out to prepare a rope. It was nearly 5:00 P.M. when Bell finished the two letters. Asked if he was ready, he replied that he was, since his life was now worth nothing, but he took the opportunity to remark, "I am only twenty-six years old."

He was asked to identify others in his gang but declined to "peach" on them. He blamed drink and gambling for his end as he walked the 50 feet to the sturdy sycamore tree, where the noose awaited, but took one last swig of whiskey when it was offered. As they put the noose over his head and adjusted it, he began to pray in a low tone, and the men simply marched away holding the loose end. Tom Bell was pulled up, and the loose end was tied off to the tree trunk. Without a drop to dislocate his vertebrae, the condemned man slowly strangled to death. Sheriff Mulford and his posse arrived ten minutes after his life was extinct and were present when the body was cut down and buried in an unmarked grave nearby.

Jack Phillips was tried as an accessory and served two years in prison. Bill Gristy was returned to prison on his original sentence but was pardoned in 1858 in consideration of his cooperation with lawmen. Smith was in and out of prison the rest of his life. Perry Owens was released for lack of evidence. All the other members of Bell's gang managed to flee the region or blend with the general population and were not heard of again.

CHAPTER TWO

BALDY GREEN—THE JEHU

There were many legendary drivers in the Old West. Every rolling stagecoach, whether a deluxe Concord or a celerity wagon, a buckboard or a surplus army ambulance, had one thing in common—the driver. Road agents sometimes made a noticeable effort to avoid a certain "sagebrush navigator." However, in Nevada during the early 1860s an odd situation developed where it seemed the highwaymen targeted a particular jehu named "Baldy" Green, or was it only a coincidence since he often had the large treasure runs.

Stagecoach drivers were known by many titles, including knight or knight of the lash, whip, sagebrush navigator, or jehu, the last being reserved for a driver who drove at a very fast pace, sometimes seeming reckless to his passengers. However, no stage driver kept his job for long if his recklessness endangered his passengers. Drivers were a hardy lot representing a cross-section of the nation's citizens. Many chewed, smoked, or cussed mercilessly, but others were kind and gentle, especially with the ladies who rode on their coaches. The stagecoach driver was captain of his vessel. He commanded all who boarded and was often admired, usually respected, and always appreciated. Not every man could handle the ribbons of a four-up or six-up through any weather on every type of frontier road, so the stagecoach driver was quite a peculiar person even by western standards.

Many times it was only the iron will and bravado of the driver that brought the coach through bad weather, across swollen rivers, over treacherous roads, with poor stock, while surviving attacks by highwaymen or Indians. One of the most notable jehus in Nevada was Baldy Green, who earned his sobriquet because he had not a hair on his head. After Green was robbed on June 10, 1868, Virginia City's *Territorial Enterprise* observed, "Baldy Green is exceedingly unlucky, as the road agents appear to have singled him out as their special man to halt and plunder, and they always come at him with shotguns."

The *Carson Daily Appeal* reported that the Pioneer Stage Line coach, driven by Baldy Green and bound for Virginia City, was stopped on a Sunday night, May 21, 1865, about a half mile south of Silver City. Three road agents armed with shotguns were afoot when they suddenly appeared and stopped the coach. No horses were seen, which would have helped to later identify the road agents, and all three men were disguised with long masks. They demanded Wells, Fargo & Company's treasure box. One of the passengers was riding beside Green while the other six passengers were inside. All were ordered out, and the robbers went through each passenger's belongings taking all valuables. Green returned to the scene the following morning, determined to find some clue to the road agents, and found two of the masks and the tracks of three horses nearby.

Wells, Fargo & Company offered a reward for the return of its money and the arrest and conviction of the robbers. Soon arrests were occurring at various places in Nevada Territory based upon the slim descriptions the passengers could provide, but none of the men proved to be parties to the crime and all were released. Two weeks passed before Charles A. "Jack" Harris and Moses P. Haines were arrested. When a writ of habeas corpus failed to gain their release, Haines began to talk, identifying Harris and A. P. Waterman as two of the men involved in the robbery.

The trial of Harris and Waterman began on August 15, 1865. The defense attorneys, according to the *Carson Daily Appeal,* were "striving their hardest to secure all the possible advantages to their clients known to the quirks and quibbles of the law." Haines, the primary prosecution witness, related the details leading up to the robbery and afterwards but insisted he was not present. He said that Harris had previously mentioned he wanted to rob a stagecoach and when Haines agreed to help, Harris told him that Waterman was in on it. Haines believed he was to take part in the robbery, but as the day neared, Harris told him it would be himself, Waterman, and a third man whose name Harris refused to divulge. Haines was to be the lookout only. Harris then spoke with a man named Low—Wells, Fargo & Company's hostler—who also agreed to help in the business.

Harris was concerned that the stagecoach might come in too late or too early and remained in Slicer's Saloon the night of the robbery and sent Haines to watch the Wells, Fargo office. The stagecoach arrived at 10:00 P.M. and stayed only fifteen minutes. Haines learned from Low that the box was loaded. After the coach left, Haines hurried to Slicer's and reported to Harris. Haines then saddled a horse for Harris and tied it to an awning post at the Penrod House, and soon Harris came out and rode off toward Virginia City by the shortest route.

Harris returned to town at 2:00 A.M. and asked Haines to put up the horse, which was heated from being run hard. Harris then related some of the details of the robbery, saying there was one robber positioned in front of the stagecoach and one on each side, so the driver had little choice but to pass down the box when asked only once. Harris said he had left the unopened treasure box with the other men. Three days later Harris told Haines that the box had contained $5,500 in coin and $4,000 in greenbacks. This was to be divided into four shares, with Haines and Low dividing one share between them. Haines got the one-quarter share from Waterman on May 30. It consisted of $1,580 in gold coins and $1,000 in greenbacks. Haines buried the greenbacks and on June 1 gave Low $800 in gold coins, cheating the hostler out of part of his share by keeping the rest for himself. Later Waterman gave him several watches, which they seemed sure could not be identified, but Haines put them into a yeast powder box and buried them in his chicken coop.

Based upon the evidence and testimony of Haines, Waterman was found guilty of stagecoach robbery and sentenced to serve thirteen years in prison. Harris was acquitted, as there was no testimony that could place him at the scene of the robbery while Waterman had been in possession of the plunder delivered to Haines. Haines and Low were not charged because they had turned state's evidence and helped recover much of the stolen money.

◇ ◇ ◇

The Overland stage that left Virginia City for Austin on September 7, 1867, was stopped and robbed in the afternoon at Desert Wells Station, 16 miles out, by three men wearing masks and armed with double-barreled shotguns. The three robbers came to the station about 1:30 P.M. and leveled their guns on the cook and hostler, the only persons about the place, and tied their hands and feet. The robbers stowed them away in a granary for safekeeping and then placed themselves on lookout for the stage.

About 2:00 A.M. the stage drove up to the barn and stopped. The lead robber stepped out and, pointing his gun at driver "Baldy" Green, told him to get down from his seat. When he came down, the leader tied him hand and foot while his partners kept their guns upon the passengers, eight in number, all within the coach and unarmed. The passengers included: Prof. Whitney, J. P. Clough, W. H. Davis, Lieutenant G. W. Walker, F. Haskins, W. Clark, S. Stocker, and a lady whose name did not appear among the departures.

Once Green was secured, the passengers were requested to come out one at a time, and in turn each was securely tied with cords taken from bales of hay. The robbers then proceeded to go through the passengers for their valuables, which amounted to $1,000, and took out the

California Company stage leaving International Hotel,
Virginia City, Nevada, headed for California

COURTESY OF THE SOCIETY OF CALIFORNIA PIONEERS, SAN FRANCISCO,
GIFT OF FLORENCE V. FLINN

wooden treasure box, which they split open with an ax to take out three bars of silver bullion. They kept the stage at the station, with the driver and all hands tied up, until 5:30 P.M., when they untied the hostler and had him harness the horses to the stage. They then placed the passengers inside and, releasing Green, told him to drive off.

When the stage was gone, they again bound the hostler and put him back in the granary. Each robber selected a good horse from the stock of the Overland Company. In lieu of saddles, they strapped on their horses blankets taken from the beds of the employees and departed. After the robbers were gone, the hostler managed to roll to where the cook was lying and place himself in such a position that the cook was able to gnaw off the cord with which he was tied, and both were soon free. The cook, a young man about eighteen years old named Austin Smith, then mounted a horse and rode to the city with the news of the robbery. He left the station about 6:00 P.M. and arrived at 7:00 P.M.

The robbers left in the direction of the Truckee River. Although it was supposed that they lived in Virginia City, one stated at the hearing of Smith that they were watching for the stage from Austin and, if they had stopped it rather than the coach from Virginia City, they would have obtained a few bars of gold bullion. Instead the robbers obtained about $1,000 from the passengers and three bars of silver bullion. After the road agents left the station, they were first seen by several parties as they ran their horses in the direction of Virginia City. They were last seen about dark at the foot of Long Valley northeast of the city, but they were not captured. One bar of silver bullion was later found and recovered, but the other two bars remained missing for five years, the value of all three being only $3,584.06. The robbers were never identified.

On November 17, 1872, J. Wright and Thomas Cocking were arrested after each had been seen in possession of a bar of silver bullion. Cocking said that he and Wright had gone out looking for the old Overland Road and, on stopping at Twelve-Mile House, built a fire in the yard. When the fire burned down, the silver bricks were exposed beneath the ashes. They took the bricks to town and tried unsuccessfully to dispose of them. Lawmen were informed and made the arrests, but the bars were not immediately found. After four hours in jail, Cocking, with some persuasion, disclosed where his bar was hidden, and it was returned to Wells, Fargo & Company. Wright's bar had been secured by the McKay brothers, who said they would turn it over to the rightful owner when identified. The bar was identified as one of three bars of silver bullion taken in a stagecoach robbery five years earlier, and it was also returned to Wells, Fargo & Company. Neither Cocking nor Wright was indicted for trying to dispose of the bullion.

<> <> <>

About 11:30 P.M. on June 10, 1868, the Overland stage coming to Virginia City was stopped and robbed in Six-Mile Canyon. It was about 5 miles from the city and just beyond the Sugar-Loaf Mountain near a bridge across the bed of the canyon. The robbers were lying in wait, and the first that the passengers knew of the matter was the halting of the stage, which was going at a slow pace. The robbers, three in number, were well armed with double-barreled shotguns, and they were completely masked by white cloths tied over their faces. One of the robbers stood at the leaders holding their reins, his gun leveled at the head of driver Baldy Green, who had twice before been stopped in the same way. The robbers ordered him to get down from his seat.

"Get out," said another of the robbers to the passengers.

"What is the matter?" asked a passenger.

"Get out—get out of there, I tell you—all of you!" was the reply. Looking at the glittering barrels of the shotguns, all understood the situation and got out.

The man who did the talking, the apparent leader of the gang, hastily searched all the men for arms and afterwards more leisurely "went through" them for valuables. The passengers included Mr. David B. McGee and his wife, Miss Susan Hodgen, Barney Dougherty, Antoine Aguayo and Dr. C. W. Heath.

From Mr. McGee they took $8.00 in coins and a common silver watch, but, not liking the appearance of the watch, returned it. They caught Dr. Heath trying to slip his watch, a very fine one worth $300, into one of his boots and confiscated it at once, also taking $300 from him. Antoine Aguayo contributed $325 and a fine chronometer watch worth $250, but he also had in a pocket memorandum book a check for $3,000, which he slipped under a cushion where it was overlooked by the robbers. Even Green was relieved of $10, but from the ladies they got nothing. Mrs. McGee had $900 concealed in the bosom of her dress, but she was only slightly searched and the money was not discovered. Miss Hodgen had a watch and some money but was not searched. Barney Dougherty, a hostler who had for some time been employed on the route, had $200 in coins in a buckskin purse. He cunningly managed, however, to slip it down the back of his neck while getting out of the coach, and it was not discovered by the robbers. They found only six bits of silver in his pocket, so mistaking him for some poor, impecunious devil, passed him by without much ceremony.

Having collected the money and valuables from the passengers, the road agents threw the mail and baggage out of the coach, but these were left unmolested. Retaining three bars of bullion, two of the road agents drove the stage up the canyon. One of the robbers who took charge of the coach was described as a man of rather slender build and about 5 feet 11 inches in height. The other was described as being rather short and slightly built.

The remaining robber, the leader, and another who spoke only a word or two in front of the passengers, ordered them all to take up their line of march to a ravine in the vicinity, telling Green to get his whip and take it along. On arriving at the ravine, the passengers were formed into a line and told to keep far enough apart to prevent their conversing with each other. Then they were ordered to march up the ravine. With the robber-leader walking behind with his double-barreled shotgun at the ready, the passengers were driven like sheep from the road up into the hills a distance of three-quarters of a mile. They were halted and ordered to sit, and the leader kept guard over them until about 1:00 A.M., sometimes standing still for a time before starting to pace again.

The leader was of medium height and heavy set, about 165 pounds, and wore a linen coat with white pantaloons or white canvas overalls. He spoke little and never once removed his mask. He stood guard until he thought his two partners had sufficient time to accomplish their work and then took out his watch and told them they should quietly remain where they were for twenty-five minutes when he would come for them with the coach. He told them that if they came down to the mouth of the ravine they would find his men "ready to attend to them," and he marched off.

After waiting and shivering in the cold for half an hour, the party started down the ravine and onto the road. On getting to the Lady Bryan Mill, McGee procured a horse and hurried to Virginia City to give the alarm, while the others followed on foot. About 2 miles up the canyon from where the stage was stopped, the coach and team were found, the horses tied to some bushes by the roadside. Here it appeared that the two robbers who drove off with the coach finished their part of the business by breaking open the treasure box and taking the contents. They got $109 and four small packages of coins and took three bars of bullion, but overlooked several packages that were in the express pocketbook.

It was nearly daylight when the passengers reached Virginia City and told of their unpleasant experience. A certain Latham of Wells, Fargo & Company and several others went to the scene of the robbery about daylight and succeeded, after a considerable search, in finding two of the stolen bars of bullion in the sagebrush near the Rogers' Mill where they had been thrown by the robbers only a short distance from the road. The third bar was not found but the leather bag in which it had been contained was recovered, and it had been cut open. Sheriff Pat Mulcahy of Storey County, Sheriff G. W. Shaw of Lyon County, and many other officers and detectives were busy the following day looking through the hills in the neighborhood where the robbery occurred and prospecting about the city. Wells, Fargo & Company offered a reward of $3,000 in gold for the arrest and conviction of the three road agents, but up to the following midnight no further traces had been found of either the robbers or the stolen property.

On June 30 Chief of Police Mark Strouse of Virginia City arrested three men who were living in Six-Mile Canyon. Their names were reportedly Andrew J. Davis, Benjamin F. Dale, and John H. Squiers, and a hearing was scheduled for the following afternoon. Green testified that the road agents who had stopped his coaches on June 10 and the voices of those who stopped him in September 1867 were similar, but he could not say that the voices of the defendants matched the voices of the road agents. On the day following the hearing, the *Enterprise* reported on the remainder of the testimony:

EXAMINATION OF THE PARTIES CHARGED WITH THE STAGE ROBBERY—Yesterday afternoon at 1 o'clock a preliminary examination of John H. Squiers and Benjamin F. Dale, charged with the late robbery of Wells, Fargo & Co.'s Overland coach, was had before City Recorder Lowery. No charge was brought against Andrew J. Davis, who was arrested with the two others . . . The principal witnesses examined were Mr. Magee and wife of Carson City, who were in the coach at the time the robbery was committed, and Baldy Green, the driver of the coach. Mr. and Mrs. Magee were quite positive that they recognized the voice of John H. Squiers as being that of the man who acted as Captain to the robbers on the occasion of the stopping and plundering of the coach; they also swore that the general appearance and walk of Squiers and Dale were the same as that of the two most active robbers on the occasion. Mrs. Magee said that the voice of Squiers was very peculiar and she could not be mistaken in it. (Both Mr. and Mrs. Magee had heard the prisoners converse in the station house previous to the examination). She also said that at one time she saw the back part of the Captain's head and that the color of his hair was a dark brown (brown black), the same as that of Squiers. She saw his head when it was very bright moonlight and also noticed that he appeared to have large chin whiskers tucked under his cloth mask. Baldy Green was quite sure also that he recognized . . . their general appearance and movements were also the same. His account of the robbery was substantially the same as that given by other witnesses and differs so little from the account we published at the time that we will not repeat it here. The men have nothing of the cast of countenance or ferocity of expression popularly supposed to characterize the highwayman. Squiers, though only of medium height, is a man of well built and firmly knit frame, with a full dark brown beard reaching down upon his breast, and is a very fine looking man. His features are regular and fine and he has very bright and expressive dark eyes, and has altogether the appearance of a man of much *nerve, self-command and extraordinary firmness, though without any look of evil. Dale is a man of slender build, with light hair and beard, thin face, spare arms and bony fingers; of a mild appearance, fine steady eyes and much self-command for a man apparently of an excitable tempera-ment. Neither of the men are over thirty-eight years of age, we should judge. Their appearance and bearing are certainly much in their favor, whatever may be proved against them—they appear in every respect capa-ble of the politeness of language and gentlemanly considerateness of demeanor displayed by the parties who stopped and robbed the coach on the occasion referred to. Squiers and Dale were held to answer in the sum of $2,000 each.*

Squiers and Dale were not indicted for stagecoach robbery due to a lack of evidence, and Dale was not heard of again in Nevada. Another gang member would later provide information that Davis and Squiers were parties to a stagecoach robbery in September 1864 and on October 31, 1866. In November 1870 the first train robbery in the West occurred near Verdi, Nevada, and one of the gang's members, a man named Odlum, would betray the robbers. He also admitted involvement in the stagecoach robbery of October 31, 1866, and named John Squiers, Andrew J. Davis, T. Cockerell and a man named Roper as his accomplices. Davis and Squiers pled guilty to robbing the train. Davis was sentenced to ten years in prison while Squiers received a sentence of twenty-three-and-a-half years, so there seemed no point in the cost of a trial for stagecoach robbery.

CHAPTER THREE

ROBBERY AT PORTNEUF

The gold rush into the Dakotas, Idaho, and Montana started a decade after gold was discovered at Sutter's Mill in California. The roads to and from the diggings went through hundreds of miles of the most desolate country imaginable, but as it happened, particular places seemed ideal for the road agents to congregate and ply their trade. These places were inevitably called a robbers' roost, and in the north this gathering place was at the northern mouth to Portneuf Canyon. When a robbery in the canyon turned deadly in 1865, Montana's infamous vigilantes became interested, tracked down the murders, and "pulled them up a tree" by their necks.

The area that would become the Dakotas, Idaho, and Montana had been inhabited by hunter-gatherer aboriginal peoples for 14,000 years. In 1742 the region was explored and claimed by France. Twenty years later it was ceded to Britain, but it was returned to France in 1800 just in time to be included in America's purchase of the Louisiana Territory in 1803. In 1805 the Lewis and Clark expedition traversed the Northwest Territory and mapped the Lemhi-Salmon and Lolo-Clearwater routes. Two years later the first fur trading post was established in the northeast region, now North Dakota, and in 1834 Fort Boise was established to the west in present-day Idaho.

French adventurers between 1807 and 1840 established a network of natural trails and passages through this rough country. Along these trails they designated certain places that were particularly well adapted to survival where water and wood, grass and game were abundant, or at least readily available. On one of these natural routes, the ninth port, or Portneuf, was at the northeast mouth of a canyon. This arid valley lay below ridges with limited timber.

Trappers and mountain men soon followed this trail searching for beaver. In 1812 British colonists tried to establish the Red River settlement at Pembrina but it failed. It was not until forty years later that Charles Cavalier established an agricultural colony at the site. In 1841 as Americans began to realize their "manifest destiny," the trek commenced from present day North Dakota west into the Oregon Country. The area experienced a great deal of emigrant traffic but little in the way of settlement.

By 1860 settlement of the region began with the influx of Americans and Europeans. It was not long before the region's rich mineral deposits were discovered in what had rapidly been transformed by dividing the Oregon Territory into the Oregon and Washington Territories. The Washington Territory was then divided to create the Idaho Territory, and the latter was divided again to create the Montana Territory.

The towns of Virginia City and Bannack sprang up over night in Montana near the rich diggings, and it became necessary to establish stagecoach service to these boomtowns. Oliver and Conover's Stage Company provided service between Salt Lake City and Virginia City in 1863, but it went out of business when Barlow, Sanderson & Company, as part of Ben Holladay's line, established a stagecoach line to bring in miners and payrolls and to take out the gold dust and other express. Ben Holladay of the Overland Stagecoach Company was awarded, on July 1, 1864, the lucrative U.S. mail contract of $13, 271 per year for four years. A stage line needed the mail contract to survive, express business to make some profit, and passengers to make the line a success, and Overland had all three.

One route, starting from Salt Lake City, went to Bear River Junction, Deep Creek, all in present-day Utah. It continued into present-day Idaho to Marsh Valley, the northeast mouth of Portneuf Canyon, and Pocatello. It crossed the Snake River at Overland Ferry near Cedar Point, then went on to Camas Creek, to Pleasant Valley, and on to Junction, Montana. From Junction, aptly named, one road led to Virginia City and the other to Bannack. Post offices on this line were located in Ogden, Fort Hall, Cache Valley, the Snake River ferry, Bannack, and Virginia City. Traveling in the southerly direction, the line divided at Marsh Valley with the through coach going southwest into Salt Lake City while another coach went west to Boise.

At the northeast end of Portneuf Canyon there was a swing station that came to be known as Robbers' Roost because it was the point on the trail beyond which the southbound treasure-laden coaches were most vulnerable to robbery, and it was at this station that robbers watched for signs of treasure aboard.

Portneuf Canyon was soon infested with road agents as it was the ideal place to rob the coaches before they reached Marsh Valley some distance south of Portneuf Canyon. It was at Marsh Valley that the contents of the stagecoach were divided, with the brass locked through mails, express, and passengers for Salt Lake City continuing on the original coach while another coach was started for Boise with passengers, mail, and express for that city.

<> <> <>

Barlow, Sanderson's Overland line was well equipped with fine Concord coaches pulled by four carefully matched mules. On July 10, 1865, loaded with the mails and seven passengers, the coach left Virginia City for Salt Lake City and Boise with Frank Williams driving and Charlie Parks riding on the left as the shotgun messenger. Aboard were: James B. Brown; Andrew J. McCausland; A. S. Parker, a freighter from Atchison, Kansas; David Dinan; Lawrence Mers; and L. F. Carpenter, a businessman well known throughout Montana. Williams and Brown were bound for Boise while the others were bound for Salt Lake City.

Several of the men had on their persons and hidden among their luggage, $65,000 in gold dust packed in cans, which at the time's rate of $13.50 per ounce weighed an aggregate of nearly 5,000 ounces. They also had among them more than $5,000 in treasury notes. The gold, which was being transported for a number of successful miners in Virginia City, was to be forwarded to the East after reaching Salt Lake City. The men, because of the great treasure in their care, were all well armed with revolvers that they carried on their persons or placed near at hand within the coach.

On July 13 at 3:00 P.M., the coach was heading southwest at a leisurely pace. The men aboard had twice seen the same suspicious-looking man on horseback pass the stagecoach. However, when nothing occurred, they relaxed a bit but still remained alert. Williams had donned a bright red neckerchief for this leg of their journey and had his hands full of reins as the coach approached a place in Portneuf Canyon a few miles past the station where the road was thickly walled with brush. The coach had just come under a projecting rock on one side and was approaching a clump of trees along the stream on the other side when a man stepped out of the trees and ordered, "Halt!"

In but a moment six more men stepped into view from the brush, and each man, with his face blackened as a disguise, was holding a shotgun pointed at the driver and messenger or at the coach. They ordered the passengers to alight, and within the coach there was a scramble as the passengers retrieved their weapons. Parker, Mers, and Dinan started to comply with the order to disembark, guns in hand, when one or more of them fired at the robbers, but without effect. The three were already on the ground when the robbers returned fire, riddling the coach with buckshot, which instantly killed Mers and Dinan, mortally wounded McCausland and Parker, and inflicted a serious but not fatal wound on messenger Parks. Once the shooting ceased, Williams jumped from the boot and Brown from the interior, and they escaped into the brush. The robbers quickly reloaded their double-barreled shotguns and fired at the fleeing pair; since Brown and Williams were already into the brush, the road agents missed their targets.

When McCausland was shot, he fell over onto Carpenter, pinning him to the floor of the coach so he could not escape and so completely drenching him with blood that the robbers thought both men were mortally wounded and would soon be dead. The road agents questioned Carpenter and Parker about the treasure before the latter breathed his last breath, but they did not disturb McCausland as he was unconscious and near death.

All the carpet sacks were rifled for gold dust and valuables, and all the cans of gold dust they found in the hind boot and passenger compartment were collected. The robbers next went through the bodies of the passengers, taking everything of value from their pockets, and then cut open the mailbags. Finally they were about to finish Parks and Carpenter, but Carpenter begged for his life so piteously and for the life of Parks, who he wanted to remain with him the short time he had to live, that the robbers relented and reluctantly agreed. The leader then called for their horses, and another man, the eighth in the party who had been holding their "fine American horses" in the brush a few rods off, brought them forward. The men mounted and rode off.

As soon as the road agents were out of sight, Carpenter jumped up, secured Parks onto one of the stage mules, mounted another, and rode several miles back to the Portneuf Canyon Station, where a pack train belonging to Carpenter was corralled. Carpenter assembled a small party of men and returned to the scene of the murders where they collected their dead, gathered the mutilated mail, harnessed a team to the coach, and returned to the station. Stage driver Bill Worley later took the mail from the station and delivered it to Salt Lake City, where Dinan's partner, Mr. Holmes, and McCausland's brother were about to depart to the Snake River to see that the bodies received a decent burial.

The frequency and boldness of robberies in the rough country had encouraged the citizens to form a vigilance committee, and they had

Barlow, Sanderson & Co. stagecoach

been active in the community for months. The members of the committee took a particular interest in the Portneuf robbery of July 13 because of the great loss of life and plunder. There had been a number of previous robberies in that vicinity, one as early as 1863, and many a man had been "pulled up a tree" or dangled from a gallows, but this had not deterred the road agents.

Frank Williams was upbraided by the line superintendent for failing to offer resistance, so he soon quit the stage line, drew his pay, and started for Salt Lake City. Brown and Williams were suspected of complicity in the robbery because, with all the shooting, neither man had suffered a scratch. However, Brown was soon cleared of involvement. A member of the vigilance committee was assigned to watch Williams and followed him through Salt Lake City and on to Denver, Colorado. Williams, over the next few months, began spending lavishly on liquor and women, going through several thousand dollars even though his total worth from his stage-line pay would have been less than $200. The Montana man sent word to his committee, and a party of men joined him in Denver.

Williams must have become suspicious because he suddenly packed his kit and started out of the territory. He only got as far as Godfrey's Station between Julesburg and Denver when, on January 2, 1866, he was overtaken and arrested. Confronted with the suspicions of the vigilantes, according to Jerome Smiley in his *History of Denver,* Williams "fell to his knees, conscience stricken, and provided a full confession." He admitted that his bright red neckerchief was a signal to the gang that the treasure was aboard, and then he named the eight men who, with him, had participated in the robbery and also named at least seven other members of the gang.

Williams identified the Portneuf robbers as members of the Picket Corral Gang headed by David Opdyke, sometimes spelled Updyke. He told where the "main body" of the murderers could be located in Colorado and revealed that it was his part in the robbery to drive the coach into the ambush in a manner that would arouse the least suspicion and then to be certain the horses did not bolt and carry the stagecoach out of danger. He had done his job well and had been paid off in treasury notes, nearly all of which he had already spent.

The vigilantes took Williams to Cherry Creek, a short distance southeast of Denver and a popular place for hangings, selected a sturdy cottonwood tree and, on January 4, pulled him up and tied off the loose end. The men pinned a drawing of a "mysterious coffin and a red cross" to his chest and left him dangling as a warning to others.

The Montana party remained in Colorado and took the trail of the other murderers, who were led by Hank Buckner. On January 18 the *Idaho Statesman* reported, "Buckner, the Road Agent, Hung—The

Vedette of the 8th says that the Montana vigilantes captured and hung Buckner and four others of the Port Neuf stage robbers a few days ago, near Denver. . . . "

After dispatching all the Portneuf fugitives they found in Colorado, the vigilantes returned to Montana and began to watch Opdyke.

David Opdyke had been born in New York in 1830. When he was twenty-five years old, he went to California where, too late for the gold rush, he took employment with the California Stage Company for two years. In 1858 he went to British America and later to Canada, but he found no opportunities and returned to California, dividing the next four years between that state and Nevada. In 1864 he followed the talk of rich mineral deposits in Idaho and discovered a rich claim on Ophir Mountain. With his profits from that venture, he bought a livery stable in Boise City, which became the headquarters for a large gang of road agents and horse thieves. Opdyke, for his share of the plunder, had supplied the robbers with horses, guns, and ammunition for their assault upon the stagecoach at Portneuf Canyon.

One of the robbers was Frank Johnson, a keeper of a road house 8 miles from Boise, but he escaped into Oregon and was later sent to prison there. The other two Portneuf murderers took their share of the plunder, fled, and were never heard from again in the territory. Most of the treasure was never accounted for since at least ten men had taken a share, a little over $6,000 each, and had six months to spend it. There may not have been anything left to recover.

Opdyke was involved in the Democratic Party in Idaho and managed to get himself elected sheriff of Ada County. He planned to use his position to dispose of the strong vigilante committee formed at the Payette Valley river settlement, since it was cutting deeply into his illegal profits. He managed to get warrants issued for the arrest of thirty men but planned to shoot down the leaders and as many others as possible, claiming they had attempted to resist or escape. The committee received notice of the plans, armed themselves, and met the posse of fifteen, outnumbering them two to one. The entire party proceeded to Boise where the complaint was dropped.

Next the county commissioners brought charges against Opdyke for defaulting on $1,100 and, to avoid prosecution, Opdyke had to pay the money, but he openly vowed revenge. In 1865 the citizens had organized an expedition against marauding Indians. Opdyke managed to be involved and embezzle much of the arms and supplies, which he cached for his gang. He also tried to get ownership of eleven pack ponies and finally succeeded, but Opdyke's attorney eventually had to pay a judgment of $800 to the rightful owner for the value of those ponies. One of the principal witnesses against Opdyke in the suit for the ponies was Reuben Raymond, a recently discharged soldier much liked in the neighborhood. On April 3, 1865, John C. Clark, in a job put up by Opdyke, murdered Raymond in the stable with numerous witnesses present. Raymond was unarmed and "shot down like a dog." Two days later Clark was taken from the guardhouse and lynched, and Opdyke again vowed revenge, swearing he would kill the men responsible. He and his men then threatened to burn Boise.

The citizens were outraged. They established a night watch and targeted the criminal element with death or banishment. Many got the word, and soon Opdyke was nearly alone but under the watchful eye of the vigilantes. John Dixon and Opdyke left town for Rocky Bar on April 12 but were separated along the way. The vigilantes followed closely and captured Dixon on the road. They took him to a cabin on Rocky Bar and arrested Opdyke, and then took both men to Syrup Creek, 10 miles further on. There they selected a tree with two sturdy limbs and hanged both of their prisoners. The remainder of the Picket Corral Gang learned of the fate of their leader, and soon there was not one of Opdyke's ruffians to be found anywhere near Boise.

Although Opdyke was not hanged for his part in the Portneuf stagecoach robbery and murders, he still met the fate that was due him.

CHAPTER FOUR

STEPHEN VENARD

In every stagecoach robbery that achieved greatness there had to be a dedicated and capable lawman. In the Old West a man was "game" if he could face death bravely, and many a man proved himself in a one-on-one confrontation. However, in 1866 Stephen Venard distinguished himself by single-handedly shooting down three armed and dangerous road agents in California's rugged mountain region and then apologized for the excess when it took four bullets from his Winchester to get the job done.

Stephen "Steve" Venard went west as soon as he learned of the gold strike in California. He tried his hand at mining but was never able to file a decent claim, though at times he did find enough gold to keep him in supplies. By late 1851 he had moved along and on October 13, 1851, wrote to his sister to update her on his situation. The bleak nature of life in the goldfields and the stark loneliness are most apparent, especially for a man twenty-eight years old:

Sis:
Having finished the task of preparing and eating my supper I shoved back the dishes took my paper, ink and pen in hand to address a few lines to

you, telling you that I am in good health and hoping these same few lines may find you and all of your relations and friends enjoying the same blessing.

I have not heard anything from you Waynesville folks for more than a year. The last I heard was about the time Grandfather was hurt on the railroad, and have not heard whether he ever recovered or not although I wrote home for them to be sure and let me know in their next letter, but I suppose it was so long before they wrote to me they had forgotten all about it. It seems to me that you are all very busy or don't think Steve worth the paper and time consumed in writing or some of you would have written before this for I have received but one letter within a year. Well let us talk a little about honey. Well I suppose you have heard all about our poor beef, ducks, and frog soup times on the plains, so we will turn over one leaf and find ourselves in the rich land on the 19th of September 1850. Well I went to work at mining and succeeded in raising enough of the precious metal by the first of Nov. to lay in my winters provision. Five of us joined and built a cabin, and there I remained until about last of Dec. Then I left for the North Fork of the American river where I remained until about the 17th of March. Thence to Indian Kenyon remaining but two weeks there thence back to the North Fork again, where I remained until sometime in May, during this time I managed to scrape together four or five hundred dollars but times appeared rather dull and I concluded to go two or three hundred miles north, where men were making their pounds per day, and after chasing those rich diggings about two months and never getting the first sight of them, I concluded they had left the country but you had better believe I came very near overhauling them having once gotten within one hundred miles of them but by the time I had made that hundred miles they had begin to squander and travel faster than I could, so I halted to see what was best to be done. On examining my finances I found that from four to six dollars per day going out and nothing coming in had reduced them to an almost empty purse, but this was no place to be idle so I turned about and went to Downieville, and finding no show there I came on to this place where I remained ever since and probably shall all winter for six weeks after I came here I tried mining and did not pay board, so I concluded that would not do, since that time I have been working by the day and job, making from six to ten dollars a day so I am about as well off as I was last fall.

Since I have been in the country I have had some experience in back life having lived for two months at a time entirely alone enjoying the solitude of a mountain life undisturbed by anything save that of the nightly prowling of Coyotes, or the almost incessant growling and squeaking of the mice as they helped themselves to the scanty morsel which was left at supper.

Write on the receipt of this and let me know how you are getting along and also our relatives and friends and most particularly the ladies for they are so scarce in this country that I had almost forgotten that there was any such angelic creatures on earth any more. And if you hear any good young housekeeper enquiring for employment just send her to me and I will pay her better wages to superintend my little house and family that she can get in the state of Ohio where she would have to perform five times the labor. It is now growing late and as I have to rise early to prepare breakfast, I will close, but first beg you to excuse my foolish writing, which I hope you will readily do when I tell you that we must resort to anything in California to pass away time. No more at the present but remain—Yours truly,

Stephen Venard

Venard was born at Lebanon, Ohio, on the Allen Kirby farm southwest of the city in 1823. When his family moved to Waynesville, he attended the old Waynesville Academy there and worked on the family farm until he got the "gold fever" and left for the West Coast. After his mining efforts failed, he settled in Nevada City and engaged in merchandising, freighting, and the cattle business, though occasionally he would take time from his business enterprises to search for gold. He had been an unsuccessful candidate for sheriff in 1860. He was highly respected by everyone, and in 1864 became city marshal of Nevada City but was replaced the following year by George Pierce.

<> <> <>

In 1866 the roads near Nevada City were infested with road agents. They robbed any person thought to have valuables, but particularly targeted the Wells, Fargo & Company treasure boxes carried on the stagecoaches between California and Washington or Nevada. The country within a few miles of Nevada City was particularly rugged terrain with steep ravines and gullies and rushing water in the creek bottoms swollen by recent heavy rains, large boulders perched precariously along the roads, trails ready to tumble down at any time, and chaparral as high as a man. Black's Crossing, later Purdon's Crossing, was near the summit on the approach to Nevada City on the south side of the Yuba River. It was the ideal place to stop a stagecoach, as the horses had to be driven at a slow walk and were tired after pulling the coach up the steep grade.

On May 6 the North San Juan stagecoach going to Nevada City, driven by John Majors, was stopped by three disguised road agents who found that the only passengers were two Chinese men. One Chinese man was flat broke but the other had $400 in his money belt, and they beat him badly when he resisted. They managed to open the Wells, Fargo treasure box only to find a solid iron box inside, and they were not equipped to open it. Majors said, "Sorry, boys, the company must have been expecting you." The leader of the robbers replied, "We'll come better prepared in the future."

Determined that their night not be a "water haul," the road agents went a few miles more and stopped the Washington stagecoach and found the pickings to be better.

As the gang began to plan its next stagecoach robbery, two of the road agents went into Nevada City on May 14 to stock up on supplies, including a cask of gunpowder. The men made camp 6 miles north of the city, not far from the summit of the road into the city, and enjoyed cigars

Stephen Venard

and brandy, taking turns of two hours standing guard. Early on the morning of May 16, they positioned themselves in the brush at the summit and prepared to meet the Telegraph Line stagecoach again. At 4:30 A.M. the San Juan coach, driven by Sam "Kalamazoo" Cooper and carrying six passengers, came lumbering over the summit with the horses at a slow walk. Suddenly the three disguised road agents leaped into the road in front of the horses, waving their arms, and ordered Cooper to stop and throw out the treasure box. The driver said, "Hello George, so it's you again." George W. Moore replied, "Well, don't ever mention my name again. I want nothing to do with you, but I mean to have that box so toss it down. I'm after Wells, Fargo. . . . " Cooper had known Moore previously and recognized him immediately.

When the box was on the road, the six passengers were ordered to disembark. Frank McKee and Ned Hatfield were relieved of their revolvers, but there was no further molestation of the passengers. Hatfield, who was known to the robbers, expressed concern that they would take his money, about $3,500 of the money in the box, and one of the robbers said they would indeed take the money, but that Hatfield would be reimbursed by Wells, Fargo as the money was in their care.

One of the robbers watched the seven men while the other two road agents took a crowbar and beat on the box, but that had little effect. They brought out the cask of gunpowder and told the driver, "We came prepared with powder this time," and then announced, "Either we get the gold this time or we'll blow the stage into the Yuba River." They carefully tamped the gunpowder into the lock and detonated it, but it had little effect. Next they tamped in a larger charge and also tamped around it mud and leaves to form a shaped charge. This blew the lock, and the men pulled out $7,900 in gold dust and coins. After the collection was completed, the robbers passed around a bottle of brandy among the passengers and enjoyed a cigar while they gathered up and threw the shattered pieces of the box into the coach. They ordered everyone aboard and told Cooper to drive on. The entire operation had taken thirty minutes.

<> <> <>

The driver wasted no time getting into Nevada City. It was 6:00 A.M. and there was hardly a soul on the street, but he pulled up in front of the sheriff's office rather than the stage office, and this attracted considerable attention. He woke Sheriff R. B. Gentry and related all the facts of the robbery. Within an hour the sheriff had a four-man posse in the saddle. His deputies included his brother Albert, James H. Lee, A. W. Potter, and

Stephen Venard. They rode to the scene and began looking for a trail. Lee and Venard found footprints leading into the brush and followed the tracks. The remainder of the posse went around to the bridge on the opposite side of the trail to wait for the two deputies to come out. When it became too rough for the horses and it seemed clear that the men meant to come out at Hoyt's Crossing, Venard sent Lee around to the bridge with his horse to meet the sheriff and other two deputies and relate this intelligence, while he continued on foot.

Venard had just come into Myer's Creek, a mile from where he left his companions, and was about to cross when he realized that one of the robbers was standing right in front of him 20 feet away and about to bring his revolver into play. As Venard brought his Henry rifle to his shoulder, he saw that another robber was a short distance above and also pulling his revolver, but he had no time to change targets and fired a single round from his Henry rifle sending a ball right through the robber's heart and killing him instantly. At the sound of the shot, the second robber scrambled behind a large boulder for cover. Venard took aim and waited. When the robber raised up to fire, Venard put a single round through his brain. The man had snapped his revolver at Venard, but it had misfired.

The deputy hurried to where the men lay and took their pistols, then searched the area and found the stolen treasure. He covered the bodies and loot with leaves and marked the spot before continuing his search for the third robber. Soon he saw the man 60 yards away trying to climb out of the ravine over a particularly steep side. Venard fired once. The man fell, wounded in his arm, but immediately got up and began scratching his way up the hill again. Venard took a second longer with his fourth shot, the second at this fugitive, and the robber dropped in his tracks. He rolled over and looked down at Venard before his head slumped, and the deputy knew his man was dead. The robber then rolled down the hill coming to rest at the bottom of the ravine.

Venard made his way toward the bridge at Hoyt's Crossing. When he stepped onto the road, he found a large body of men milling about and asked what had happened. He learned that Wells, Fargo's agent Bill Davidson had posted a $3,000 reward for the robbers, dead or alive. "Well, you better all go home," Venard told them. "They are all dead." The sheriff was incredulous, so Venard guided him back to Myer's Creek and showed him the bodies. While there, they collected the stolen treasure. They checked it over and found the loot $20 short. The posse then returned to town, notified the coroner, and by 2:00 P.M. had returned the stolen treasure to the Wells, Fargo & Company office. Coroner W. C. Stiles quickly assembled a jury and went to the scene of the killings. After a careful examination of the battleground, they recovered the bodies, taking nearly four hours to get them to the nearest point on the road since, at times, the bodies had to be dragged. The jury returned to town for the inquest and to identify the bodies.

The leader of the gang, and the first man killed, was identified as Jack Williams but his real name was George Shanks. He had been born in New York and had been a pressman on the *Tribune* before going to California in the early 1850s. He tried to live within the law taking jobs in mining, ranching, cooking, and writing. He had once held a job with a stage line but was fired for trying to rob a passenger and was sentenced to serve a term in California's San Quentin Prison. He enlisted in Company G of the Fourth California Infantry in 1861 but deserted after two months. He was captured but again deserted in early 1862. In 1864 he was working as a cook in Nevada City under the alias Billy Smith when he tried to kill his employer, William Barton, after a disagreement over pay. He fired through a window but only managed to wound his target. He then went to Colfax where he soon got into another shooting scrape. To avoid arrest, he next drifted into Grass Valley, settling a few miles from Nevada City. There he got into a squabble with the owner of Unger's Saloon, but could only find the saloon keeper's son and beat him badly. The boy swore out a warrant for Shanks's arrest, but when officer J. D. Meeks tried to arrest Shanks, he held off the lawman at gunpoint and escaped. He then adopted the alias Jack Williams, the name of a desperado hanged in 1856, and from that time on concentrated on robbing stagecoaches. He came to be known by victims and lawmen as the "ghost of Jack Williams" and lived up to that name by appearing and disappearing mysteriously on many occasions. When the body of Shanks was searched, they found the missing $20 gold piece, so that the entire stolen treasure was returned to Wells, Fargo & Company. They also found a gold watch and diamond ring taken from Sam Henry in a robbery that had occurred several weeks earlier.

The second man killed was Robert Finn, sometimes spelled Flynn, alias Caton or Katon and Kerrigan. He was also a deserter from the army and an escaped convict from California's prison. He had tried his hand at mining, but when Williams talked to him of the riches to be found in the Wells, Fargo treasure boxes, he joined the gang.

The third man killed, and the one requiring a second shot, was George W. Moore. Moore, when examined, was found to have a boot on one foot and a shoe on the other, necessary as he had broken his ankle in a mining accident at the mining camp of Rough & Ready just before he joined the Williams gang. This suggested that he might not have been with the Williams gang for very long. When Moore was searched, the coroner found two photographs pinned inside his shirt over his heart, showing his wife and children. One man said that he knew Moore previously and that Moore had also spent a term in California's prison, but that he did not know the crime Moore had committed.

Venard was given a great deal of renown as a result of his actions and was offered the entire reward. He insisted that he would only take his fifth share, but finally agreed to half at the insistence of the other posse members. He apologized for the wasted bullet and would only take reimbursement for three rounds. Sheriff Gentry appointed him a regular deputy and assigned him to Meadow Lake. Wells, Fargo also presented him with a gold-mounted and inscribed special model Henry rifle. Governor Frederick F. Low appointed Venard a lieutenant colonel in the National Guard and cited him "for meritorious service in the field." He then took a position with Wells, Fargo as a shotgun messenger and then for a short time served as a guard on the Central Pacific Railroad's pay car.

Stephen Venard died of kidney disease in the county hospital in Nevada City on May 20, 1891. He was described as a "man of modest demeanor, thoroughly temperate, of the strictest probity and not afraid of anything." He died so poor that his friends had to take up a collection of $70 to pay for his burial.

CHAPTER FIVE

THE INNOCENTS

The criminal justice system of the Old West lacked the sophistication of today, but lawmen and judges tried their best to punish only the guilty. However, when capable, devious men carefully planned and executed a "frame-up" innocent men could find themselves behind prison walls. Three Oregon men learned this for themselves in 1872, and it took several years to expose the conspiracy, refute the perjurious testimony, and gain their freedom from the prison at Salem.

On Friday, July 12, 1872, C. N. Thornbury and two companions were traveling by buggy through Antelope Canyon about 65 miles from The Dalles and about the same distance from Canyon City in the northeast part of Oregon. They were about 5 miles from the Tompkins spread, a few miles past H. Moppin's place, and still 5 miles from T. M. Ward's Station when Thornbury saw two men on the ground not far off the trail. Each man was armed with a rifle or shotgun, but no horses were seen. Anticipating trouble, the three travelers took out their pistols and laid them close at hand, but they passed by the suspicious-looking footpads without incident and had almost forgotten them until the stagecoach caught up with Thornbury at Ward's Station.

The topless stage wagon from Canyon City to The Dalles, driven by Ad Edgar, was thirty minutes behind the Thornbury party and 5 miles from Ward's Station when it reached Antelope Canyon at 6:30 P.M., a half hour before sunset. Antelope Canyon was a deep hollow about a mile long, very rocky throughout with heavy brush at some places. The country around was prairie and comparatively flat, but the sides of the canyon were very steep and the road through the canyon was also quite steep in places.

The stage had been traveling up one of the steep grades with three of the passengers walking closely behind to relieve the horses of the extra weight. The passengers walking included two men and a boy, while teacher Mary Morrison, who had boarded with her son at the Burnt Ranch Station 36 miles previous rode inside. Moppin's granddaughter, Miss Lizzie Franklin, rode. A man known only as Captain Fearing sat next to Edgar on the driver's seat.

Suddenly three men thoroughly disguised with masks of blue cloth stepped out of the brush on the right side—two were 6 feet tall and one was of average size. The smaller man shouted, "Halt! Throw up your hands." Mrs. Morrison cried out, "My God, we are all murdered." Edgar said, "Hello! Oh my God!" The average-sized man, apparently the leader, responded, "Mr. Edgar, we will not hurt you. We only want the mail." The two tall men passed around the front of the coach, one taking the reins while the other covered the passengers with his shotgun. The leader was holding a short-barreled Henry rifle, the robber at the reins was armed with a Henry rifle of a standard barrel length, and the third man used a double-barreled shotgun.

Once his men were in position, the robber-leader demanded that the mail and express be thrown out, but Edgar kept hold of the reins and let Captain Fearing do the work. Miss Franklin was sobbing the entire time. Mrs. Morrison got down when the coach stopped and took her boy behind the coach for protection in case shooting started.

After the sacks were thrown down, the gang leader ordered the driver to continue on. Morrison then asked the robbers to allow her and the boy to board the coach. The leader replied, "Get in, babies," and they climbed aboard.

Edgar took special note of a distinctive pearl-handled revolver in the belt of the leader. Miss Franklin said much later, after considerable prompting by her grandfather, that she had noticed red hair showing from beneath the mask of one of the robbers, freckles on his hands, and blue eyes. All heard the voice of the leader, but there was little else to help identify the robbers.

The coach continued to Ward's station and from there hurried on to The Dalles, arriving on Saturday evening. Two Wasco County deputy sheriffs left the next morning to investigate the scene, arriving at Ward's Station on Sunday night. It was too dark to begin so they stayed the night and left for the scene at daybreak on Monday. On the way, they met Moppin, whose house was about 1 mile from the mouth of the canyon on the Canyon City side and fewer than 3 miles from Tompkins ranch. With him were John Attleberry and Billy Cantrell. Moppin said that he and C. Adams had gone to the scene of the robbery the previous morning and found several trails of foot tracks and horse tracks. Moppin directed the search for the sheriff's party and pointed out the foot tracks, including a very distinctive boot print, and then, after traveling about 3 miles, found where the horses had been tied. He pointed out one print that was long and slender as of a mule, sometimes called a "hoof bound," and another distinctive print that was the large round track of a shod American horse.

The five men searched the area and found trails leading to and away from the scene. The party then traveled the road in both directions 30 miles and, though they were not able to find any place where the robbers had left the road, Moppin found several masks made from a saddle blanket, which he gave to the sheriff with much ceremony.

He suspected Frank Tompkins, a well-to-do cattleman, so they went to his ranch, where Moppin almost immediately selected two horses grazing nearby whose tracks matched exactly those of the tracks at the robbery scene. An iron-gray horse, about the size of a cayuse horse, was the source of the small, narrow shoe print, while the other was a bay mare, which made a large round shoe print. They removed one of the shoes from the iron-gray horse for a comparison, which they found matched exactly the tracks they had followed from the scene. They next made a careful search of Tompkins's premises and found half a saddle blanket belonging to Tompkins in a barn, which was exactly like the two masks found near the crime scene. The left boot of a pair of boots they found in Tompkins's loft was an exact match for the boot prints they found near the scene of the robbery. They learned that the boots belonged to William Bramlette.

Moppin later claimed that he was deputized to arrest Bramlette. He said that he went to Coleman's cabin on Trout Creek with Attleberry, Cantrell, and Cantrell's son, Garret, and arrested Bramlette. After traveling 4 miles, Moppin sent Cantrell and his son ahead while he and Attleberry took Bramlette off the road 300 yards from the creek, to a level bench on the side of the mountain, where there was a large juniper tree. The two men said they told their prisoner that he was running with bad people and that he, Moppin, was going to hang them as quickly as he could catch them. He said he scared Bramlette so thoroughly that the prisoner agreed to confess and said he always looked upon Moppin, the man who had just threatened to hang him, as a father.

According to Moppin, Bramlette then provided a detailed confession of every detail of the robbery implicating Tompkins, Hanson, and White. What Moppin failed to mention, however, was that they had strangled their prisoner to extort the confession and had demanded answers to leading questions that required only a nod or a "yes" answer. Bramlette had been "pulled up a tree" at least three times and held aloft until he was unconscious before being dropped. Before the fourth hanging, Bramlette was threatened with being tied off and left to strangle to death. Moppin and Attleberry later told lawmen that their prisoner had provided a description of the horses used, and, conveniently, they were the exact animals that Moppin had identified when the sheriff's party went to Tompkins's pasture. Once Bramlette was safe in the house, with others present, he recanted his confession.

<> <> <>

On Friday Moppin, Attleberry, Cantrell, Samuel Porter, William Quinn, and W. C. Hale went to a certain Grater's one-room log cabin on Trout Creek. They tied their horses 100 yards from the house and crept up, where they found Tompkins tying his horse to a wagon. He was surrounded and arrested at gunpoint. When told the charge was robbing the stagecoach, Tompkins said, "I am clear of that charge, and can prove myself clear by Hanson and White, and by my wife."

When Moppin replied that Hanson and White would not be competent witnesses as he was going to arrest them also, Tompkins said, "If that is all, it don't amount to much."

Moppin then told Tompkins that he had Bramlette and told of his confession, to which Tompkins reportedly replied that Bramlette was scared or crazy. The prisoner was taken to Moppin's place by Porter while Moppin and the others went on to Tompkins's place, where they arrested Ed Hanson. When Hanson said White had gone to the valley to look for horses, Moppin sent Quinn and Attleberry after White. They returned with their prisoner in two hours, and the entire party went to Moppin's to await the return of a lawman.

A deputy sheriff had gone to The Dalles, a town in northeast Oregon, to swear out warrants for the arrest of Tompkins, White, Bramlette, and Hanson. On his way he met a deputy U.S. Marshal, and they went to Antelope Canyon together. When the deputy sheriff arrived, he learned of the arrests of the suspected robbers and of the detailed confession of Bramlette, the particulars having been recorded by Moppin and Attleberry, who had forced the confession from Bramlette. As the lawmen did not have room to take in four prisoners in their buggy, they took White, Hanson, and Tompkins to The Dalles where they were lodged in the county jail. Bramlette was left at Ward's station and brought down by James Cunningham on The Dalles boat two days later.

The U.S. Grand Jury met and indicted all four men on a single true bill charging them with putting the life of the mail carrier in jeopardy when robbing the mails, a charge that was punishable by life imprisonment. The legal maneuver of a single indictment prevented Mrs. Tompkins from testifying and corroborating the alibis of White, Bramlette, and Hanson. It was the strategy of the defense that once these three defendants were exonerated by her testimony, they could testify for Tompkins and clear him of the charges, but when Tompkins's wife was prohibited from testifying, the men were left with no alibi, excepting their self-serving claim of innocence.

The defendants were brought to trial in Judge M. P. Deady's Circuit Court on Monday, August 20, 1872. The trial lasted six days, their alibi testimony was dismissed by the jury, and the four men were convicted entirely on circumstantial evidence. Much of the testimony of Moppin and the other men interested in conviction and rewards was refuted by disinterested parties whose testimony must have been disregarded as well. In addition, several decisions by the judge appeared quite prejudicial against the defendants. The jury was only in deliberations for fifteen minutes, and upon the rendering of their guilty verdicts, a motion was filed for a new trial. Judge Deady denied the motion and sentenced the four defendants to terms of life imprisonment at hard labor in the state prison in Salem.

Ad Edgar, the driver, Sheriff J. M. Boyd of Baker County, and Wells, Fargo & Company's agent H. C. Page were certain the four men were innocent and kept a watch for any clue that would lead them to the guilty parties. One strong factor in their belief was that when the four men were arrested none had a pearl-handled revolver, and it was shown that none of the four men had ever owned one. Tompkins had used nearly all his property and wealth in defending the case, and when he was delivered to the prison, his wife became a charity case.

<> <> <>

Frank Johnson, alias Fulford, was serving a term at the Oregon penitentiary on another charge when he encountered Boyd, who was at the

A poster advertising the Oregon Stage Line

prison on other business several years later. He told the lawman that a man named Homily, whose real name was Milton Shepardson, along with T. D. Phelps and Charles Darnell, were the men who had robbed the Canyon City stagecoach on July 12, 1872. He said that he was going to participate, but his wife would not allow it so he withdrew. He did, however, know enough of the details to convince Boyd that he was telling the truth. He said that Shepardson and Darnell met Phelps, the Gemtown blacksmith, and tried to convince him to replace Johnson, as they wanted three men to do the work. Phelps declined until Shepardson returned in a few days and described the plan. Shepardson said he had picked the spot and described the role each man would play. Since it seemed foolproof, Phelps agreed to take part.

Johnson said that after the mail sacks were thrown out and the stagecoach was ordered to drive on, the robbers loaded the matter on a pack animal and rode all night. They went into camp at daylight and searched all the matter, burning everything with no value, and then divided the plunder. Shepardson went to Lewiston, Phelps went to his ranch near Dayton in Walla Walla County, Washington, and Darnell went to Iowa Hill, Placer County, California.

Boyd was soon on their trail, and arrested Darnell and took him to Portland. He next went after Phelps. Realizing he would need substantially more evidence to get a conviction and secure the release of four innocent men, he hinted that Shepardson was in jail and was about to "peach" on his confederates. Phelps then made a detailed confession and would later turn state's evidence in court to gain his release.

<> <> <>

Meanwhile in Baker County, Oregon, Deputy Sheriff William Harpe arrested Shepardson at Sparta, Oregon, and took from him a derringer and a distinctive pearl-handled revolver. He was charged with the robbery of a Shasta County, California, stagecoach on the night of August 21, 1871, when five road agents shared $4,300 in gold bullion and coins.

Shepardson was not charged in a September 26, 1871, robbery of the same stagecoach at the same place, where the same five men only shared $160, but it was after that second robbery that two members of the gang were captured and Shepardson fled into Oregon. Shepardson posted $2,400 bail on the Shasta County charge and was released but returned for his trial in March 1872. His defense was that he was in Oregon during a long period before, during, and after the robbery. He proved his alibi through false testimony. Shepardson was convicted but granted a new trial based on an error. At his second trial he was again convicted and again granted a new trial on an error. Following the third trial, he was acquitted; the jury finding him "guilty, but not proven," and he was released.

On January 26, 1876, Deputy U.S. Marshal Boyd arrested Shepardson in his Colusa, California, hotel room. Shepardson had been working on his brother's farm 13 miles from town but had come into Colusa that day. The warrant had been issued for Mathews, an alias he was then using, but Shepardson denied he was the wanted man. Since Boyd had the forethought to include a "John Doe" on the warrant, Shepardson was taken into custody under that name. He was taken to Portland on the steamer *Ajax,* where Boyd was assisted by a deputy U.S. marshal.

Shepardson's trial was called in the U.S. Circuit Court on June 21, 1876, and he was confronted with his alibi testimony in the California case, where he had proven he was in Oregon at the time of the Canyon City stagecoach robbery. There was strong evidence of his guilt, but Judge M. P. Deady directed the jury to return a verdict of not guilty because conviction was barred by the statute of limitations. Still, the evidence was sufficient to gain the release of the four innocent men then in prison. President Ulysses S. Grant signed a full pardon, and the innocent men were released on November 6, 1876, after serving nearly four years of their life sentences.

Shepardson was almost immediately arrested on a charge of robbing a stagecoach in Baker County, Oregon, in 1873, and this crime was not barred by the statute of limitations. He was convicted and sentenced to serve ten years in the Oregon State Penitentiary. He was admitted on

November 13, 1876, and registered as prisoner 693. He served his time as a model prisoner and was released on August 23, 1883. He lived a law-abiding life thereafter, or at least was never again convicted of a crime. He died at his home in Peanut, California, on November 14, 1915.

<> <> <>

In 1872 Tompkins had been a well-to-do cattleman in the vicinity of Antelope Canyon and, possibly because he was a major landowner and powerful force in the community, he had a number of neighbors who were envious and desired his downfall. It was clear afterwards that Moppin and others gave perjured testimony and manufactured physical evidence in a conspiracy to incriminate four innocent men. During the trial Moppin testified that he had known Tompkins for many years and in several places and had good relations until Jack Mount was killed at the Tompkins place. Soon after the killing of Mount, Moppin was sued by the French & Gilman Company, and he blamed Tompkins for instigating the action against him. The litigation was over an unpaid note and Moppin said he did not ask Tompkins to be his security on that note, but when the note was produced it showed that Tompkins had signed for his neighbor and would have become liable if not for the suit.

Moppin later denied, as stated in testimony by one witness, that he said of Tompkins when at The Dalles, "I will send him to Hell if I get the chance."

Moppin testified that when Tompkins was arrested, the prisoner said that he had always treated his captor well, and Moppin responded, "You played me a mean trick in the matter with French. French never refused to trust me for goods, for I was always good on my contracts; my property always made me good." This corroborated Tompkins allegation and showed Moppin was motivated by revenge in implicating his former friend, but Moppin and his conspirators were never prosecuted for their crimes.

CHAPTER SIX

THE BOISE BANDITS

Modus operandi, or mode of operation, are the distinctive features of a series of crimes that link them together and prove that they were committed by the same perpetrators. When lawmen of the Old West investigated stagecoach robberies, they assumed that if a robbery was repeated by men of similar description, at the same place, at the same time of day, and in the same manner, it was the same gang of thieves. When nearly identical stagecoach robberies occurred near Boise, Idaho, in late 1875 and early 1876, detectives were at first certain they were looking for one gang of road agents. Through careful investigation, however, they were surprised to learn that they had three different gangs, and that none of the members of each gang knew members of another.

Stagecoach robbery was a crime of choice because the coach could be stopped some distance from any population center, thus allowing time for the robbers to flee before a posse could take the field, so it was peculiar to have a stagecoach jumped within sight of town. But just such a fate befell Boise City's stage to Silver City repeatedly in the 1870s.

The reason behind the several robberies of the Silver City coach was that, of the three coaches leaving Boise, it was most likely to carry

treasure, and the robbing at the same time of day was the curious practice of having three coaches leave Boise at about the same hour, each
driving in rotation the 75 yards from the post office in the Overland
House, where they picked up the mail, then to the Northwestern Stage
Company office to pick up their passengers. The Umatilla coach went
first at 3:00 A.M. and then departed. In about ten minutes the Silver City
coach finished loading and started out. Next came the Overland coach,
which started about ten minutes after the Silver City coach. This strategy, it was thought, might prevent robbers from having enough time to
accomplish their work with one coach clearing the way in advance and
another coming just behind. The robbers, however, knew of the schedule
and were game to try robbery anyway.

On November 10, 1875, the Silver City stage, driven by Charley
Downey, was stopped just after 3:30 A.M. not more than 1½ miles south
of Boise City. Three road agents demanded and received Wells, Fargo &
Company's treasure box, and the mails were also taken. The robbers
were disguised and carried double-barreled shotguns. They got
$7,069.19 in gold bullion, dust, and greenbacks. The driver wasted more
than seven hours because he went on to the Sixteen Mile House before
he sent someone back to Boise City with a report of the robbery. It rained
hard between the time of the robbery and its report in the city, so no
tracks were visible when the lawmen arrived at the scene, and there
seemed to be no leads.

Wells, Fargo & Company's detective, John N. Thacker, was put on
the case, but it was not until May 1876 that Thacker was able to arrest
five men, including the three highwaymen named George Bouldin, John
Souder, and John Lee. Driver Charles W. Downey was arrested for complicity in the crime, and James M. Trask was jailed as an accessory before
and after the fact for "running" (melting) the bullion to change its
appearance. The men were indicted and tried for stagecoach robbery in
December, but the jury could not arrive at a verdict. A motion was filed
for a new trial. On December 19, 1876, the grand jury returned indictments against the prisoners for grand larceny, a lesser charge.

On February 2, 1876, long before the arrest of the November 10 robbers, the Silver City stagecoach driven by Tom Huston was stopped south of the city again at about 3:30 A.M., this time just before crossing the first bridge, which was only one-half mile below the city. The highwaymen demanded the treasure box, but this time refused to take the mail. The box contained $35 in gold coins and $240 in currency and the express mail. Like the first robbery, the *Idaho Statesman* reported this to be "the boldest robbery in this part of the country." Within two days Sheriff James D. Agnew, Marshal Joseph Pinkham, and their deputies had arrested the Henderson brothers and four others they thought involved. Eventually all the prisoners were released except Steve J. Henderson, who was twice tried for stagecoach robbery and finally acquitted in December.

On April 19, 1876, the Silver City stagecoach was again driven by Charley Downey and got off on time, ten minutes behind the Umatilla coach and the same amount of time ahead of the Overland coach. The stagecoach had four passengers including Division Agent Andy Baker, stage driver Ed Paine, and Mrs. Charles Adams inside, and outside with the driver was Francisco Soto. It was a bright night and the frost reflected the starlight, but the lamps were also lit. When the coach arrived at the first bridge, one-half mile south of town, a man appeared almost in front of the horses with gun in hand and sang out, "Halt!"

The team had slowed as the horses were about to step onto the bridge and suddenly stopped at the command. At that instant another man appeared in the door of the old vacated ferry house and called out in a guttural tone, an attempt to disguise his voice, "Throw out that box."

The box was under some luggage in the boot, and this delayed the driver, so the road agent, apparently anxious at the prospect of the arrival of the Overland coach, called out his command again. The box was thrown off, and then the stage was ordered to drive on. The Overland coach passed the spot on schedule. The passengers saw nothing suspicious and first learned of the robbery when they got to Fruit's Ferry House at the second bridge one-quarter mile beyond. Baker and

Paine got off the Silver City coach at the ferry house and, with Mr. Fruit, went back to the scene of the robbery. However, they could find no trace of the robbers.

Later the scene was examined by W. B. Morris, superintendent of the line, Sheriff Agnew, and Deputy U.S. Marshal Pinkham, but no trace of the robbers or any clue at all could be found. The box was found broken open, the catch of the padlock having been cut off with a cold chisel, but the box had been empty so the robbers got nothing for their trouble. The *Idaho Statesman* announced that this was "the boldest of the three robberies."

On Monday, April 25 at about 3:30 A.M., the same two road agents stopped the Silver City coach one-half mile south of town, the same place as before. There had been so many robberies close to one another that a signal had been arranged: If the stage was robbed, the driver, as soon as he was over the first bridge and out of danger, was to fire a single shot in the air. He was then to continue on his route. Men had been assigned to take up positions to watch for anyone coming into town from the south, and others were assigned to go directly to the scene and try to find evidence and track the robbers. Still other trusted men were to be awakened and to begin a systematic check of certain persons suspected by the lawmen.

Billy Ridenbaugh, agent at the stage office, was just buckling the last strap on the boot of the Overland coach when the shot was heard. Tom Morrow and several others were standing about the stage office, so Ridenbaugh called to Fred Epstein to watch the office while he started on a run for the bridge, with Morrow close behind. They were at the scene in less than ten minutes and were soon joined by several others who had hitched a ride on the Overland coach as well as the general route agent, who was on the Umatilla coach when he heard the shot, jumped off, and ran back. Mrs. Pinkham heard the shot and woke her husband, the deputy U.S. marshal. The town was closed up with heavy patrols on the south end, so there was no possibility of anyone going in or out without being seen. Although the men at the first bridge found

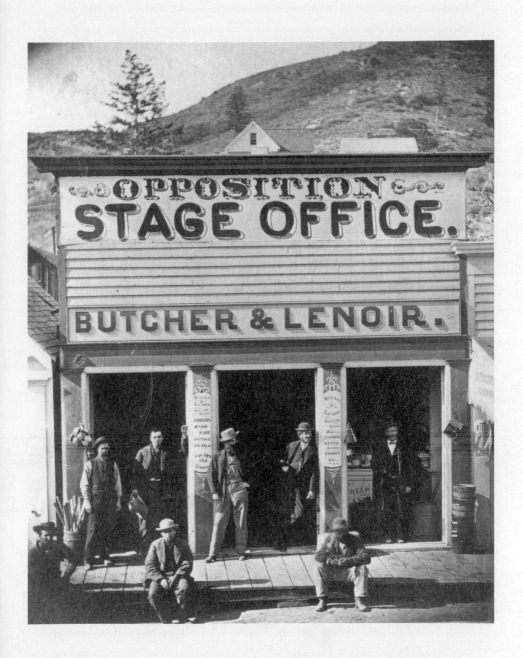

Opposition Stage Office, Silver City, Idaho
IDAHO STATE HISTORICAL SOCIETY, 77-19.1

nothing but the box broken open and the contents rifled, this box had contained no treasure, so the robbers got nothing for their trouble.

At daylight Sheriff Agnew, Marshal Pinkham, Undersheriff Joe Oldham, Bill Noyes, Joe Davis, and others followed tracks they believed were the robbers'. They followed the trail across Tom Davis's orchard, and then waded through the slough, and, where the wet tracks came out, followed a clear trail to the road. One man's track was large and the other very small. The robbers' foot tracks showed they sometimes ran as if they thought they were being pursued. They went through John Krall's field and then above the old burying ground, but there the trail went onto hard ground and could not be followed further. It appeared that the two men planned by a circuitous route to circle the town and come in on the north side, but most of the effort at catching a glimpse of them had been concentrated on the south side of Boise, as it was thought the robbers would take the shortest route into town. The night had been particularly dark and a man could not be distinguished if more than a few rods off, so the few patrols on the north had seen nothing.

On Sunday a man strongly suspected to be one of the robbers, John W. Miller, was arrested and lodged in the prison. He made a full confession, which was written down by A. L. Anderson, clerk of the district court. Present at the interview was Marshal Joe Pinkham, stage line Superintendent William B. Morris, and Judge M. E. Hollister. Sheriff Agnew learned from Miller's confession that the other robber was Talton B. Scott, and it was Scott who had done all the active work at the previous two robberies of April 19 and April 25, both of which were "water hauls."

All day Sunday Scott lay hidden away in his camp among the lava rocks within an hour's walk of the city, and from this vantage point, he watched the officers and citizens who were traversing the plain in every direction. On Sunday night one of the alert searchers saw a light among the rocks, but it was put out before anyone could get close enough to pinpoint the location. On Tuesday hunger and the need to find out what happened to his partner forced Scott to come into town. Awaiting an opportunity to search for Miller, he hid beneath the Baptist Church, where he was discovered on Thursday.

A man named Gilman, who was mixed up in the later movements of Scott, acted as a decoy to try to get the fugitive to surrender while Undersheriff Oldham, Deputy Sheriff Cutter, and Deputy Marshal Pinkham covered the building. Scott did not respond to Gilman's coaxing, so Sheriff Agnew called out to Scott to surrender. When he received no answer, he called out again, "Come out Scott, I want you."

At this urging, which left no doubt that the lawmen knew he was there, the fugitive crawled out and was ordered to throw up his hands. He was bound, relieved of a revolver and knife, and then led to the penitentiary. Gilman, in consideration of his cooperation and absence at the scene of the robberies, was released.

<> <> <>

The *Statesman* interviewed Scott and learned that he had come from Plattsburgh, Missouri, or at least still had relatives living there, and had received letters from that address at the Boise post office. The editor described Scott as:

a young man of medium size and height, and apparently about twenty-five years old. He is physically as fine a specimen of young manhood as we have ever seen. His features are regular and classic in their outline, presenting a model for the most critical and fastidious artist. A head shaped with all the requisites for the 'dome of thought,' and covered with hair of a rich brown, while his 'goatee' and unshaven beard is of a lighter hue. His eyes are large, somewhat prominent, blue in color . . . he is decidedly the handsomest man in Boise City.

The newspaper also gave a brief description of Miller as "a medium sized man with black hair, black eyes and dark complexion. He is rather common-place . . . we shall not stop to tell how ugly or homely he is."

On Tuesday the two prisoners were taken before Judge W. W. Glidden and charged with the robbery of February 2. They waived examination and were held on $3,000 bail to answer at the next term of the grand jury.

After Scott was in custody, one of his camps was found on the banks of the Boise River. There they found mufflers for his feet, a brown mask that would cover his head and face, a shotgun heavily loaded with buckshot, a loaded revolver, a good-sized hatchet, a knife in its scabbard, and other conveniences including blankets and picket ropes. The camp was found just before the river overflowed its banks and the *Statesman* said:

Now that Boise River has cleansed the scene by washing away the old toll house, thus making future robberies impossible, and other important and satisfactory changes having been made which promise to provide a good supply of State's evidence for the trials . . ."

In early May Scott obtained a case knife and was sawing away at the iron bars of the trap door above the jail when he was discovered by Undersheriff Oldham. Scott was then heavily shackled to prevent his escape, but boasted, "If I could get a few tools, I'd soon get out of this wooden box."

Apparently he got his tools because on Sunday, July 10, at 7:00 P.M., Scott and Miller made their escape. The prisoners were kept on the lower floor of the building. In the upper floor, separating the prison room from the one above, which was occupied by the jailer, there was an iron grating fastened with strong iron bolts. Since he was unshackled, Miller was able to stand upon the benches and, passing his arm through the grate, unscrewed two of the bolts from above and then tore the grating off by breaking the remaining bolts. In the jailer's room they found a Spencer rifle and shotgun, which they took. They passed out of town by way of the alley between Main and Idaho Streets, crossing Seventh Street near the Central Hotel and keeping in the alley until they reached Lemp's brewery.

A posse led by Sheriff Agnew spent Sunday evening trying to locate the escapees. The posse was worn out by noon, but had Scott and Miller surrounded at the head of Ruby Gulch, 8 miles northeast of town. Wells, Fargo agent Morris and Undersheriff Oldham took five men and went there to help the sheriff. They met Baldwin returning to town for supplies, and he gave them all the necessary particulars of the situation. It took two hours to reach the summit in the midst of dense chaparral country. After searching for two hours, the group retired to a wood camp for food, but suddenly a shot was heard and the men rushed to the scene. They found Undersheriff Oldham where he had been lying and watching; he had captured Miller and the Spencer carbine. Oldham reported that Scott had gone in the opposite direction when he fired, so the men scattered, began to listen for someone breaking through the brush, and systematically searched the area. In half an hour they had surrounded Scott, who called out, "Well, boys, you've got me. I've got to give in." They returned to the wood camp, finished their meal, and then took their prisoners back to Boise, arriving in town at 6:00 P.M.

<> <> <>

Benjamin Anderson began working on making the jail more secure. He laid new floors and sealed the roofs and sides of every cell with heavy matched flooring. The interior and exterior logs had been filled with cracks, which had provided the prisoners with hiding places for bits of iron and tools, but the improvements now made it impossible for them to hide anything large enough to cause damage or help in an escape. The work had been ordered when T. L. Tyner took charge of the jail during the first week of October and heard Scott, during the night, sawing at his heavy shackles. In the morning he and Sheriff Agnew examined the irons and found that they were nearly sawed through, but their search turned up nothing with which he could have done the work.

The prisoners were taken to the penitentiary while the renovations were completed, but, by the first week of November, they were back in their jail cells awaiting the December term of the district court. On December 6 Tyner had finished his duties for the day and took a stroll downtown. Sheriff Agnew decided to keep watch in his absence and heard the sounds of men working on the grating door. When he rushed in, he found that Scott and three others prisoners had nearly picked and pried off the lock of the door. They had acquired a medium-sized ax, a small bar of iron, and an old pocketknife. The sheriff believed he knew who had passed these items through the grating to the prisoners and warned, "They had better keep away, as everything goes from this on."

On December 19 the grand jury found indictments against Talton B. Scott and J. W. Miller for stage robbery and trial was set for December 23. The trial took only a few days and the two men were convicted of the charges. Miller was sentenced to serve five years at hard labor, and Scott was sentenced to serve seven years at hard labor. The two convicts were familiar with the penitentiary, having spent several weeks there during their time awaiting trial, but now they were delivered there to serve out their terms.

CHAPTER SEVEN

THE SHOWDOWN

Stephen Venard had proved his courage in 1866, but that was a battle with rifles in rugged country with plenty of cover available. In 1877 another lawman would prove he was game when he stood face-to-face at point blank range with a desperate road agent and, in an Old West–style showdown, shoot it out—a situation often portrayed but seldom true. Perhaps most remarkable, Joseph Wiley Evans had only one arm, yet this "handicapped" deputy U.S. marshal would capture more deadly desperados than any man in Arizona's early history. One can only wonder if the outcome of the showdown would have ended differently if the second road agent had not gone to collect their horses a few minutes earlier.

The town of La Paz, Arizona Territory, seemed to spring from the earth when gold placers were discovered nearby. The town was located on the Colorado River and became a popular place to cross, so the road west through Arizona became known as the La Paz Road. In 1861 and 1862, the river overflowed it banks flooding the surrounding areas, which affected the course of the river. On a February morning in early 1863 the residents of La Paz awoke to find that the fickle river had changed its course overnight and moved some distance from the town.

In March most of the residents moved south and established a new town on the east bank of the river, which they named Ehrenberg. This new town became a busy river port and the western end of Arizona's La Paz Road.

<> <> <>

On May 12, 1877, Sheriff Edward F. Bowers of Yavapai County was transporting Mary E. Sawyer, a demented woman, to the California Asylum for the Insane in Stockton via stagecoach when he had the opportunity to witness a stagecoach robbery firsthand. Three masked men stopped the stagecoach westbound for Ehrenberg when it was 2 miles west of Wickenburg in Maricopa County. They took $457 and a pistol from the sheriff, but failed to find several other packages of money he was transporting.

Opening and examining the Wells, Fargo & Company treasure box, the robbers found inside several bars of bullion bearing the stamp of Assayer Blake, which were being shipped to San Francisco by C. P. Head & Company. They cut open the mailbags, rifling and badly mutilating the contents. The mail was later collected and returned to Prescott to be "fixed up for a new start." Frank Luke, the only other passenger on the stage, surrendered his wallet containing $65 in currency and an order on parties in San Francisco for $250 more. The robbers returned the order, as it was useless to them. Satisfied that they had all Luke's valuables, they failed to search him further and missed $340 in gold coins he had in his pockets. The woman was not molested. The sheriff reported that from their physical characteristics, voices, and gestures, he believed he recognized them but did not know their names, and would be able to identify the robbers if captured. He communicated as much of the description as he could throughout the territory.

During the early evening hours of May 16, 1877, Thomas Brophy and John Sutton slipped quietly into Ehrenberg, too late to board the ferry that would carry them across the Colorado River into California.

Pencil sketch of Ehrenburg, Arizona Territory
ARIZONA HISTORICAL SOCIETY, TUCSON

They left their horses in the corral at the east end of town and stowed their tack and gear. It would be dawn before the ferry ran again, and their aim was to be as inconspicuous as possible as they passed the hours ahead. By daybreak they sensed they were being watched and had become suspicious. The men moved up the main street, which ran east to west between the river dock on the west and the town's corral at the east. They were going to retrieve their horses, but an apprehensive Brophy stopped in front of Mill's Saloon to watch the street behind them. Brophy's partner, Sutton, went ahead to collect their gear and horses and bring them back to Mill's Saloon.

Joseph Wiley Evans, line superintendent for the California & Arizona Stage Company, had recognized the men as soon as they had appeared in town. Since he had received a good description of the men forwarded by Sheriff Bowers, Evans was sure these two were the right birds. Throughout the night, Evans and Colonel J. Bryan considered the best way to arrest the two robbers without a fight and had decided to confront them as they boarded the ferry, while their hands were filled with gear and reins. But now that plan was afoul as the robbers had become cautious, so the two men approached Brophy and demanded his surrender. Bryan had armed himself with a shotgun while Evans sported a six-shooter on his right hip. Brophy had only his six-shooter, his rifle being among his gear at the corral.

Evans and Bryan watched Brophy's hands to see if they went up or down. They went down—and just a bit too fast for Evans. Brophy fired the first shot, the bullet glancing off Evans's forehead just above his left eye. Bryan immediately let loose both barrels, but he had not checked the load of his borrowed shotgun and the small shot, which struck Brophy in the face and right arm, was not enough to knock him down. Evans, hardly able to see because of the blood gushing into both eyes, got off his first shot. The bullet struck Brophy in his wounded arm, and he went down from the force. Three men "stood game," firing at each other until Brophy's pistol emptied. Brophy, unable to reload because of his wounds, then lay still as bullets whizzed over his prone body.

Sutton had returned as far as Salado's Saloon and was firing at Evans and Bryan with a Henry rifle. O. Mercer, a stage driver on Evans's line, then tried to come to the aid of Evans, but before he could get off a shot, he was hit in the shoulder with a rifle ball and went down in the street. Faced with rapid fire from a sixteen-shot repeating rifle, Evans and Bryan retreated behind the Ehrenberg Hotel while Sutton backed into Salado's Saloon. The exchange continued for several more minutes until Evans called for Sutton's surrender. Seeing that there was no hope of rescuing Brophy or making his own escape, Sutton stepped out and grounded his weapon. The entire battle had lasted fifteen minutes, more than sixty shots were exchanged, and three men were wounded. Both robbers were then arrested and a search of their gear revealed the bars of gold bullion taken from the express box.

This was the Wild West, and men, good or bad, who faced death bravely were much admired. Yuma's *Sentinel* newspaper said of them:

Good pluck was shown by all parties and none showed any signs of flickering. . . . Many thanks are due to Messrs. Evans, Bryan and Mercer for their noble conduct in this affair; few men are thus ready to risk life to arrest thieves. Would that we had more men of such promptness in Arizona. The wounded robber is dangerously shot, having nearly a pound of lead in his right arm and in his head. Mr. Mercer, the driver, I understand, is doing well, his wound being only a flesh one. Major Evans does not mind his, only on account of the girls not liking to have his handsome face marked.

In the fight, Evans, who would later become one of the most respected, yet controversial, lawmen of Arizona's territorial period, favored a six-shooter because he could not manage another. Evans had lost his left arm in 1875 in another shooting affray. In mid-February of that year, Evans had had a disagreement with James Carroll, a driver for the California & Arizona Stage Company, which led to a face-to-face shoot-out. Carroll was killed, and within a month Evans's arm, shoulder, and breast had become inflamed. As soon as the inflamation was resolved, the arm, at a very definite line of demarcation below the elbow, began to decay. It was amputated in mid-March by Fort Whipple's post surgeon Dr. Henry Lippincott at the point where live flesh met dead to save Evans's life. Evans had captured Arizona's first stagecoach robbers in January 1877, and in 1878, as a deputy U.S. marshal, escorted falsely accused stagecoach robber and Arizona pioneer John W. Swilling to Yuma for trial at the circuit court. He then captured the real robber, clearing Swilling's name three weeks after he had died in jail.

In March 1882 Evans was the man who met the Earps in front of the Porter Hotel and informed them that Frank Stillwell, "armed to the teeth," was laying an ambush at Tucson's train depot. In 1883 he failed to stop the lynching of stage robber Joe Tuttle and accessory Len Redfield in Florence.

Evans, over a decade, arrested more desperadoes than any man in Arizona, and at one time had a dozen post office rewards pending. He retired from law enforcement in 1887, opened a successful real estate firm, and died suddenly in Phoenix in 1902. Perhaps Sutton and Brophy had dismissed, or at least underestimated, the danger posed by this one-armed man of the law.

At first Sutton and Brophy identified themselves as the Johnson brothers, but later Sutton, who had come through the shoot-out unhurt, gave his true name. He was then mistakenly taken to Prescott, seat of the Third Judicial District but, when it was shown that the crime occurred in the Second Judicial District, he was immediately brought back to Ehrenberg where he boarded a steamboat for Yuma, and the court met for that district. Yuma's *Arizona Sentinel* newspaper reported on June 9th:

When being brought back here he [Sutton] made quite a little circus on board the steamboat. He threw overboard all the dishes within his reach and tried to throw a Chinaman after them, but for his heavy irons he would have succeeded. Both are still ugly and defiant. But the most mystery surrounds John Mantle. He is recognized as one of the men who committed the last stage robbery and had Sheriff Bowers' pistol in his possession. The proofs of his complicity are clear but J. A. Stewart, Supt. of the C & A Stage Co. is said to claim him as a detective in his employ. Employees of the C & A Stage Co. speak of Mantle, if without affection at least not without sympathy. Habeas Corpus has failed to affect his release and he will probably remain in jail until the December term of the Court determines his exact status. So far stage robbery in Arizona has proved unprofitable, not a single offender having escaped.

The wounded robber, Brophy, remained at Ehrenberg where, on July 4, he had his right arm amputated above the elbow by Dr. Leonard Y. Loring. The newspaper reported on July 7 that he was recovering quickly and was "up, dressed and singing." The doctor had "staid [*sic*] with him five days and nights and is entitled to even more credit for his untiring fidelity to his patient, than for the consummate skill displayed to treatment." Prescott's *Arizona Weekly Miner* reported:

The case of the supposed mail robbers, Sutton and Brophy, has become already notorious, not only throughout this Territory, but from the occident to the rising sun. Sutton was tried by a jury and ably prosecuted by H. H. Pomeroy, H. N. Alexander, and Colonel B. O. Whiting of Los Angeles, and defended by C. W. C. Rowell of San Bernardino, and an attorney from Prescott. The trial and consideration lasted four days and the jury was discharged standing six and six. The defendants, Brophy and Sutton, under the advice of Rowell, and against the solemn protest of their other attorney, plead guilty to the lowest crime known to the law under the indictment, and were sentenced to five years in the Territorial Prison, where they are now.

The curious part of the evidence was given by John Mantle, who claimed to be a detective for the postal service. This is what the U.S. Grand Jury of the Second Judicial District said about Mantle's "detective experiment":

In examination of the robbery cases of the United States mail, a state of facts was brought to light which in the opinion of the Grand Jury is deplorable in the extreme. We find one John Mantle, while in the service and under the authority of the Postal Service Department of the United States, planning and executing a robbery of a stage and of the U. S. mail.

We find that he was sent to this Territory and appointed Director to work up the facts concerning stage robberies and bring to justice the perpetrators of any stage robberies which might occur within the Territory. Mr. Mantle came here heralded by secret letters to two or three stage agents, but without notice to a single U.S. official within the Territory and no officer, either of the United States or the Territory, was ever informed of his intentions.

We find that in the town of Prescott he, with others, planned to rob the stage passengers and mail traveling from Prescott to Ehrenberg. That his plan was put into execution whereby the passengers were robbed and placed in jeopardy of their lives, and the mail was broken into and robbed.

The different stage agents along the road of the contemplated robbery were notified, but neither the passengers nor the stage driver knew what was coming.

Ed F. Bowers, sheriff of Yavapai County, was one of the passengers.

The robbing was committed a few miles from Wickenburg, and the stage agent—Pierson—of that place knew at the time the stage reached his office what was to happen, yet neither Mr. Bowers nor the others were told a word so that they might have provided for what was coming, and to save their effects and perhaps secure the robbers.

The robbery was committed under cover of guns and pistols, and the least motion of resistance by any of the passengers might have led to loss of life of one or more of the passengers. As it was, all the money had by the passengers was taken from them—some four hundred and fifty dollars from sheriff Bowers, and valuable letters mutilated and destroyed. The money taken has never been returned by the Postal authorities or anyone else.

The Grand Jury cannot too severely condemn this light-handed experiment of the Detective branch of the Postal Service and its execution, showed in the opinion of the Grand Jury, an almost criminal lack of common sense.

The Grand Jury went on to find that John Mantle had instigated the robbery "through his peculiar intellect." They said of Sutton and Brophy: "There are many unfortunate people in the world who, through poverty and destitution, might be led by a stronger will to the commission of crime and who, untampered with, would honestly struggle on."

John Sutton and Thomas Brophy were delivered to the Territorial Prison at Yuma on November 21, each to serve a five-year sentence. Sutton, who had been born in Missouri, was described as aged twenty-seven, 5 feet 4 inches in height with hazel eyes and light hair. Sutton could read and write. Brophy had been born in Tennessee, was twenty-four years of age, 5 feet 6 inches in height with light gray eyes and light-colored hair. He, too, was literate. Sutton was registered as prisoner no. 18 and Brophy as no. 19. Both men were released on May 23, 1882, after having served their sentences. Brophy was not heard of again but Sutton took on a new partner—Miguel Lavadie.

Sutton and Lavadie robbed a drunk named Louis Baker who, the day following the robbery, died of congestion of the brain from a blow to the head received during commission of the crime. The two prisoners were held to answer after Lavadie made a full confession. Both men managed several escapes from jail but were caught each time, and Sutton finally ended back in prison.

The stagecoach robbery of May 12, 1877, was the second involving undercover Postal Detective John Mantle, sometimes spelled Mantel or Mentel, who was the third robber in this adventure. The first instance of his undercover efforts resulted in the arrest and trial of Charles Bush in San Francisco, the robbery taking place at Indian Wells, California. Mantel never returned the $457 taken from Sheriff Bowers at Wickenburg, nor the money belonging to the Post Office, and retained $25 stolen in the Indian Wells robbery, which belonged to the editor of Prescott's *Weekly Miner* newspaper. Postal Agent Adams stated that Sheriff Bowers had overstated his loss and then went to Yuma for the trial. Testimony of the two robbers confirmed the amount stolen, but Adams returned to California after the trial and Bowers was never reimbursed. Mantle was released from custody several times on the order of the U.S. attorney general and the third stagecoach robber went to California, where it was inferred he would remain until he spent all his loose change on whiskey. John Mantle was not heard of again in the Arizona Territory.

CHAPTER EIGHT

THE MAN WHO SWALLOWED A WAGON WHEEL

It was rare that any road agent would try to capture a stagecoach single-handed, but that was the *modus operandi* of William "Brazen Bill" Brazelton near Tucson, Arizona Territory in 1878. He eluded lawmen by a variety of ingenious methods, but when it came time to surrender or die, he was shot full of holes before he could get off a shot. For decades afterward Tucson's superstitious citizens saw Brazen Bill's ghost haunting the road near where he was killed. Brazelton got his start as an Arizona criminal at Prescott the previous year.

Lieut. John G. Bourke, Indian ethnologist and General George Crook's biographer, was in Arizona campaigning against the Apaches with General Crook when he visited Prescott and observed:

Of all those on the southwestern frontier (Prescott) preserved the distinction of being thoroughly American. Prescott was not merely picturesque in location and dainty in appearance, with its houses neatly painted and surrounded with paling fences and supplied with windows after the American style—it was a village transplanted bodily from the centre of the Delaware, the Mohawk, or the Connecticut valley. Its inhabitants were Americans; American men had brought American wives out with them

from their old homes in the far East, and these American wives had not
forgotten the lessons of elegance and thrift learned in childhood. . . . The
houses were built in American style; the doors were American doors and
fastened with American bolts and locks, opened by American knobs, and
not closed by letting a heavy cottonwood log fall against them.

Bourke noted that the homes were furnished with cottage furni-
ture, carpets, mirrors, rocking chairs, tables, lamps, and all other appur-
tenances, "Just as one might expect to find them in any part of our
country excepting Arizona and New Mexico."

<> <> <>

It was to the dainty American town of Prescott that William Whitney
Brazelton came in mid-1876 and announced he would put on a show for
the entertainment-starved populace. A majority of the residents of
Prescott were "waiting for the wagon," seeming to live from day to day
just hoping for something to happen. Brazelton had come into Arizona
as the proprietor of a remarkable traveling show, so it was no stretch of
credulity when he advertised that his troupe would perform in Prescott.
What surprised most residents was his announcement that during their
performance he would "swallow a wagon wheel."

On the date of the event the house was filled beyond capacity by
residents intent on "seeing the elephant"—something so wondrous it
had never before been seen nor heard of. The thought of a man swallow-
ing a wagon wheel captured the imagination. Brazelton was slightly over
6 feet tall and weighed over 200 pounds, a huge man by nineteenth century standards. If any man in the Arizona Territory could do it, Brazelton
assured them, he was that man. He collected money at the gate and then
announced that his troupe had just arrived and were "making their toilet." Seeing how anxious the crowd had become, Brazelton said he would
excuse himself to hurry the players along, announcing that the show
must proceed with all due haste.

How long the people waited before they realized they had been duped is not recorded, but they never saw Brazelton again in Prescott. No person had lost more than the price of a ticket, so everyone had a good laugh and went about their business. With characteristic western humor, this "Brazen" Bill Brazelton became known as "the man who swallowed a wagon wheel."

◇ ◇ ◇

Brazelton made his way south to Tucson where he took a job in the stables and corrals, which, though well below his capabilities, had certain advantages. It was not a particularly desirable occupation so he could leave whenever he wanted, stay away for weeks, and return to find his job waiting. This gave him the opportunity to begin his career robbing stages, so he created a costume and devised a peculiar method of operations that he debuted on September 27, 1877.

At 6:00 P.M. a stout-built road agent stopped the coach from Prescott when it was 8 miles from Antelope Station in Yavapai County. The lone highwayman was dressed in old laborer's clothes, his pants tucked into his boots as a stable hand might, and he wore a mask of black gauze. He was armed with a shotgun but held a revolver so close to the barrel that it appeared tethered. He ordered the driver to dismount and hold the leaders by the bits and then ordered passengers Gus Ellis and Dan Thorne to disembark, smash open the treasure box, slit open the mailbags, and remove all the valuables. He then ordered everyone aboard and sent the coach on its way. In this stagecoach robbery, Brazelton took $600 from a registered package, a package of gold dust and bars valued at $1,300, another with $470 in currency, a letter worth $100, and other items totaling $150.

The robber next appeared in New Mexico where he stopped several coaches, the last one near Cook's Canyon east of Silver City on May 19, 1878. A civilian going by the name "Colonel" Willard and Lieut. Frank West were on the coach. This robbery was committed at night, and the

A photo of Bill Brazelton taken after his death
ARIZONA HISTORICAL SOCIETY, TUCSON

report stated that the robber "had a pistol strapped to his gun." He made off with three bars of bullion, the last he would not take when he discovered its great weight and the near impossibility of converting it into currency without raising suspicion. The peculiar method of operation had Brazelton's mark on it, and the only change was that he had replaced the flimsy black gauze with a more durable mask with eyeholes cut and a red mouth sewn on. He was cool and jocular during the commission of the crime, but it was difficult to say how much of his performance during each robbery was showmanship or serious business. One certainty, his past experience with entertainers enabled him to alter his appearance enough to make witnesses vary his height by several inches and his build by many pounds.

Tired of the long trips to find fertile stage roads, Brazelton realized that there were enough treasure-laden coaches near home to satisfy his needs. He was determined to find a place near Tucson and recruit assistance in keeping his horse and getting supplies. He chose the ranch of David Nemitz. This young man, well thought of as an honest man, would later relate how he unwillingly became an accessory to the robberies. Nemitz said that he had worked in James Carroll's corral but had recently left that employment and taken up residence beyond James Lee's flouring mill several miles south of Tucson. Brazelton called on Nemitz one day and merely asked a couple of questions and then left, but Brazelton returned the next day and asked for a confidential conversation, which was granted.

That first day Nemitz said he did not recognize the man nor did he the second time until informed. He said, "I saw before me a former fellow-laborer in the corral when Mr. Leatherwood owned it. I says, 'You look like a hard game,' and the reply was, 'You bet I'm a hard game,' and then he told all about his robberies. I was then in the power of a man who placed little value on his own or any one's life, and I felt obliged to obey the robber's commands."

Brazelton did not waste any time. On August 2 the *Arizona Citizen* wrote of the "Bold Stage Robbery" by a lone highwayman northwest of Tucson. John P. Clum, owner and editor of *The Tombstone Epitaph,* was a passenger on the stagecoach and said of his experience:

This editor has frequently read of the daring deeds of fierce highwaymen and several times within the last six months it has been necessary for us to describe the bold operations of these desperadoes, but never until day before yesterday have we had the good fortune to witness the modus operandi *by which these members of the shotgun gentry extract the valuables from a stage coach and passengers by the simple but magical persuasive power of cold lead.*

The stagecoach left Tucson on Wednesday at the usual hour of 2:00 P.M. Arthur Hill was driving and J. P. Clum, one Chinese man, and a veterinary surgeon named Wheatly were the only passengers. When they reached the ranch at Point of Mountain, 18 miles northwest of Tucson, at 5:00 P.M., a light rain was falling. Ten minutes later the stagecoach struck the wet sand at the Point of the Mountain, and the horses took a slow walk. Suddenly someone leaped from behind a bush and in rather harsh tones accosted the driver, who stopped the coach. A tall form in a mask then appeared at the left side of the coach. Covering everyone with a Spencer rifle and a six-shooter, he commanded them to remain where they were at the peril of their lives. Clum had a pistol, but it lay on the floor of the coach. Wheatly had one also, but it was on the seat under a blanket. The attack was in open daylight and had been so unexpected that the passengers were wholly unprepared, and, once under the cover of the robber's arms, everyone was quite willing to obey.

The road agent ordered the passengers to "pungle up" and, after the collection had been taken, remarked that someone in the party "looked like a sick man." No doubt he could have been speaking of any one of them. After scanning the coach for a moment, he ordered Hill to drive on, an order that he obeyed. Just as the coach started, the robber extended a very polite invitation for any of the men "to come back and fight as soon as they felt disposed to do so." The express box had been empty and there was nothing of great value in the mails, so Brazelton only obtained $37. His booty was so small that it was supposed he would soon find it necessary to rob another coach, and passengers and officers were warned to be careful.

Tucson's *Citizen* newspaper described the robber in a separate article:

So near as we remember the man who robbed the stage on Wednesday afternoon, was about six feet high and well built. He had his pants in his boots and wore small brass spurs such as are used by the army. His face was covered with a muslin mask having opening for his eyes only. His weapons were a Spencer carbine and a Colt's army size six-shooter. When making the attack he held his gun to his shoulder all the time and his pistol leveled in the fingers of the left hand closed close to the gun-barrel and parallel with it which gave it the appearance of being fastened to the Carbine.

The editor had been correct in predicting that the road agent would strike again. On Thursday, August 14, the same lone highwayman stopped another stagecoach. The *Citizen* reported, under the headline "Here We Are Again," that the stagecoach left Tucson with two passengers and with Arthur Hill again driving. John Miller, one of the passengers, was sitting next to Hill, and as they neared Point of Mountain, he asked the driver to show him just the place where the coach was robbed on July 31. Hill replied that it was only a short distance ahead and he would point out the spot. "There," said Hill, "the robber was hid behind that bush . . ." and Miller nodded. "And there he is again," shouted the driver with the same breath as the same masked robber sprang from behind the same bush and pranced about before the horses shouting, "Yes, here I am again. Throw up your hands."

The mail sacks and express box were thrown out as ordered, and the man on the inside lost only $8. Miller was obliged to give up his pocketbook, which contained $226. The stage arrived at Desert Station just about dark, and parties immediately left for Tucson to notify the authorities.

The strangest bit of evidence from these two robberies was that the tracks of two horses were at the scene of the crime but no tracks left from there. Finally a tracker named Juan Elias, the same man who led the Camp Grant Indian massacre in 1871, determined that he would solve the mystery. It happened on this second occasion that the robber's horse threw a shoe, creating the odd impression of an animal with three shod hoofs traveling in one direction and the fourth unshod hoof in the opposite direction. Elias backtracked the hoof prints to their source and found the robber's horse in the corral of David Nemitz. On examination Elias found that the robber had developed a way to turn the horse's shoes around. The shoes had been made especially for this purpose with four nail holes on each side of each shoe so accurately spaced that, when the shoes were reversed, nails could be pushed through the ready-made holes in the horse's hoof. All that remained was to turn the nails down and cut the clinchers.

Elias reported his discovery to the sheriff, so Nemitz was arrested as an accessory, as there had clearly been only one man at the scene of the robberies. Bail was set at $2,500. Nemitz said he would tell all if he could be protected from this dangerous man and then said that he allowed Brazelton to keep his horse in his corral and provided food and water when the stage robber went out on to ply his trade.

He said, "Owing to the facts in connection with my own arrest and the search going on, I feared Brazelton would suspect me of treachery and kill me. If the Sheriff's posse fails to kill the robber, my own death will soon follow."

He warned the sheriff that the man would not be taken alive unless by artful strategy and remarked, "No other man could have a stronger desire to have Brazelton killed than myself." Nemitz had disclosed that Brazelton was leaving that night to commit another stagecoach robbery and would be weighed down with all his arms.

Pima County Sheriff Charles A. Shibell summoned Marshall Buttner, R. N. Leatherwood, Charles O. Brown. Charles T. Etchells, Jim Lee, and Ika O. Brokaw as his posse to capture Brazelton. From all that Nemitz told the sheriff he deemed it necessary to shoot Brazelton on sight and so instructed his deputies. The plan was for posse members to sneak out of town one at a time and assemble near the mesquite log where Brazelton was to meet Nemitz, who was to provide the robber with supplies for the next day's work.

When Brazelton arrived at the log, he had upon his person two belts filled with cartridges, two six-shooters and a Spencer rifle. He approached the log cautiously and gave the signal, a cough, which was returned by a posse member. He then placed his hat on the log to signal Nemitz to come to him. Something alarmed Brazelton and he leaned over the log as if to look on the other side. One of the posse members was concealed there, and the silence was broken by the blast from a shotgun. A fusillade of pistol shots followed immediately and Brazelton exclaimed, "You s__ of a b___," as he fell. He lay there in the darkness, and the posse heard him gasp, "I die brave; my God, I'll pray till I die," but all he managed aloud was a rasping wheeze.

The posse remained silent, listening carefully in the dark for any sign that there was fight left in Brazelton. Finally they surrounded the prone figure and lighted matches, then counted ten holes they had deposited in Brazelton's chest between his shoulders in the area of his heart and lungs. The ambush had been so sudden that the desperado had been captured and mortally wounded without the opportunity to fire a single shot at his captors. The sheriff searched the body and discovered that Brazelton had in his possession the hood described in previous robberies and in his pockets was some of the loot, including a pair of distinctive earrings and a gold watch. The remainder of the plunder, particularly all the money, was believed to be buried somewhere south of town but was never recovered.

Ika Brokaw went to town and procured a wagon. Brazelton's body was then taken into Tucson, tied upright in a chair, displayed at the courthouse until the inquest. It was then photographed and buried the following afternoon. Prescott's *Daily Miner* reported on Brazen Bill's death:

Brazzleton [sic], *the man that single-handed commanded on many occasions 5 or 6 of the bravest Arizonians to throw up and yield over their spare funds, when shot, exclaimed, "I die brave; my God, I'll pray till I die." It was rather brave to ask forgiveness of God after having robbed an Arizona editor. He robbed, died and prayed single-handed.*

Brazelton was described in the Prescott *Enterprise* as "the most successful single-handed highway robber of modern times," and then announced, "Who he was and whither from will soon become clear, we suppose." In 1902 John P. Clum, Indian agent, postmaster, and editor of *The Tombstone Epitaph,* said that he had recently visited the grave of Brazelton a short distance from Tucson and reported,

Billy Brazelton was born in San Francisco. He was early left an orphan and made his home in an old boiler, the remains of a wreck on the 'Barbary coast.' He attended the public schools of San Francisco, became a hoodlum and killed his first man in a row when he was but fifteen years old. He robbed nine coaches in Arizona and New Mexico single-handed. Once he was closely pursued by a posse near Silver City, New Mexico when he managed to separate them and killed them one by one as they came up. He was dextrous with firearms and had no streak of yellow in him.

<> <> <>

That would seem to be the end of the Brazelton saga, but Brazen Bill was not yet finished. Twenty years after Bill's death W. C. Davis of Tucson spoke of the stage robber at San Jose, California, as reported in San Jose's *Evening News:*

The Indians and Mexicans, particularly the old people of the latter race, will never go past a place after dark where any tragedy has ever been committed, or which has been given the reputation of being queer when it has been given out that any one has seen things. Yet there is a place not far from Tucson where it is said they will not pass after dark, if they have to make a journey of a mile to go around it. The incident which put a hoodoo on the spot occurred some twenty-five years ago. . . . The spot where the highwayman met a tragic death was avoided after night fall by the Indians and Mexicans and even now some of the old timers, who remember the affair, will not go past the place in the dark, and will recite stories of how a phantom highwayman is seen standing in the road, just as Brazelton was halted on the night of his death.

CHAPTER NINE

THE IRONCLAD STAGECOACH

Deadwood was just booming in 1875 when the Cheyenne and Black Hills Stagecoach and Express line began carrying large shipments of treasure to the Union Pacific Railroad depot in Cheyenne, Wyoming. Stagecoaches had been robbed many times near Deadwood those first two years, and driver Johnny Slaughter was killed, but that gang had moved south into Nebraska in 1877 and robbed a train. The gang that filled the void and plagued the stage line thereafter worked the route to Cheyenne some 100 miles south of Deadwood, well inside Wyoming with the northern most point at a place called Robbers' Roost.

In response to the repeated attacks, the stage company lined a coach with iron plates and sent an army of shotgun messengers along with large treasure shipments as a precaution. In October 1878 three shotgun messengers awaited the arrival of the treasure coach on the trail just above Robbers' Roost while three other messengers were aboard the Monitor stagecoach when they were surprised by an attack at Canon Springs Station, still many miles north of Robbers' Roost. Five road agents made off with the treasure but not before they had killed a passenger in the attack. The murder outraged the citizens, and eventually all but one of the robbers, and several other road agents, would be killed and four-fifths of the treasure recovered.

General Phil Sheridan, to have greater control over the Dakota Territory Indians, was promoting a military command within the Black Hills. The Black Hills had been set aside for the Indians since 1851; the establishment of a military post would have been more than just an intrusion, it would have been a violation of treaties. In 1868 the Dakota Territory was divided, creating the Wyoming Territory, and on July 2, 1874, General George A. Custer was dispatched from Wyoming with a thousand men to make a reconnaissance of the Black Hills in the Dakota Territory. When the party camped near Harney's Peak, miners Horatio N. Ross and William McKay took the opportunity to search for the gold that had been rumored to lie in large quantities throughout the hills. They soon returned to their camp on French Creek with a small quantity of the yellow dust, and scout Charley Reynolds started for Laramie, the nearest town with a telegraph, to report the discovery. Word spread quickly, and soon men were invading the hills, and more were carefully planning how they could circumvent the military troops positioned to prevent a rush.

Within weeks so many men had flocked to the area of the discovery that the town of Deadwood seemed to spring up overnight. It was soon apparent that some means of travel was necessary to bring men to the new boomtown and to take out the mineral wealth they had already begun to accrue. Experienced stagecoach operators John T. Gilmer, Monroe Salisbury, and Mathewson T. Patrick saw an opportunity and established the Cheyenne and Black Hills Stage and Express Company. On April 5, 1876, the first coach of the new line left Cheyenne for Deadwood. Soon after, an organized gang of stagecoach robbers began operations, and something had to be done to protect the treasure.

Each stagecoach in the Cheyenne and Black Hills line was named, and the *Monitor* was selected to be outfitted as a special treasure coach. Previously coaches carrying treasure were standard Concords carrying a wood or iron treasure box. In early 1878 Gilmer, Salisbury, and Patrick hired A. D. Butler of Cheyenne to reconfigure the *Monitor,* and he lined the body of the coach with $5/16$-inch steel plate, which proved to withstand every rifle bullet fired at 50 feet. There were two firing ports on each side to allow the messengers to return fire when the coach was attacked. The roof was not lined because tests showed that the heavy metal placed there made the coach top heavy and prone to overturn. A specially built safe, called the "Salamander" because of its green color, was guaranteed to withstand a break-in for twenty-four hours and was securely bolted to the floor. The safe had been used during 1877 but had never been taken by road agents, so, in fact, it was untested. The coach was completed and put in service the end of May 1878 and was the only "ironclad" until the Johnny Slaughter coach began service in September.

<> <> <>

The promise of great riches did not draw every man into the Black Hills to dig for gold. Some men preferred to wait along the trail at some isolated spot and take their riches from a stagecoach. Almost as soon as the coaches began to operate, the road became infested with road agents. A large number of robbers, who seemed to be organized into a loosely affiliated gang, generally struck the southbound coaches at night between Robbers' Roost and Hat Creek. Traveling north from Hat Creek was Mays Ranch and then Robbers' Roost. Beyond this vulnerable section was Jenney's Stockade. Twelve miles beyond was Beaver Creek, and 8 miles from there was the Cañon Springs Station, 37 miles south of Deadwood, where William Miner was the stock tender. The Deadwood to Cheyenne coach sometimes carried treasure in excess of $100,000, in addition to the personal valuables of travelers.

On September 18 Cheyenne's *Leader* announced that the down coach would be transporting a quarter million dollars the following day. This practice of notifying the road agents of large treasure transfers caused great concern for the stage operators, but the *Leader* argued that it was only reporting the news that interested its readers. On September 24, 1878, two men robbed the mail coach from Fort McKinney and took $300 from two passengers. Two days later the same coach was jumped and, anticipating armed guards after the first robbery, the gang of road agents had brought a dozen men. The mails were gone through, and the two soldiers guarding the coach lost their firearms and horses.

Meanwhile at the Cañon Springs Station, events were unfolding that would change the situation in the area for months to come. During the afternoon of September 26, the *Monitor* was loaded with three ingots of bullion valued at $17.50 per ounce. One ingot, which weighed 248 ounces, was valued at $4,300, the second valued at $3,200 weighed 183 ounces, while the third ingot valued at $2,000 weighed 115 ounces. There were also 1,056 ounces of gold dust valued at $13.75 per ounce, for a total value of the dust at $14,500; jewelry valued at $1,000, half of which was a bag of diamonds; and $2,000 in currency—bringing the total value of the treasure to $27,000. The coach was driven by H. E. "Gene" Barnett and had three shotgun messengers guarding the safe— Gale Hill was on the boot with the driver while Scott Davis and Eugene Smith rode inside.

A lookout in Deadwood hurried ahead of the coach to inform a small band of road agents that the coach carried treasure. Although the *Monitor,* by policy, did not carry passengers, the line had made an exception on this run and carried Hugh O. Campbell, an operator for the Black Hills Telegraph Company who was to take over the telegraph at Jenney's Stockade 56 miles south of Deadwood. Campbell would disembark long before the coach reached Robbers' Roost. Messengers Jesse Brown, Boone May, and Billy Sample had been on the up coach but had disembarked at the Beaver Creek station and waited there for the down coach to pick them up on the down leg.

The Cañon Springs Station consisted of a stable with small living quarters for one employee. Shortly before the arrival of the treasure coach, a man on horseback rode up to the station and asked for a drink of water. Upon dismounting, he got the drop on William Miner and ordered him to throw up his hands. The stock tender was unarmed, so he had no choice but to comply. He was locked in the grain room of the stable. Soon four more road agents joined their comrade, and together

Horse-drawn stagecoach near Deadwood, South Dakota
DENVER PUBLIC LIBRARY, X-21855

they made preparations for the arrival of the *Monitor.* They knocked the earth chinking from between the logs of the stable near the door to make gun ports facing the place where the stage always stopped for the change of horses.

The stage pulled to a stop in front of the stable on schedule at 3:00 P.M., ready for the change of horses that normally delayed them about seven minutes, but the stock tender was nowhere to be seen. Gale Hill called for Miner, but when he got no answer he got down from the boot and placed a chock block under the back wheel. He then started for the stable, and at that moment the robbers opened fire. Hill was wounded in the left arm in the first volley but managed to fire back with his right hand and mistakenly believed he wounded one of the robbers. He continued to shoot and mistakenly believed he had wounded another when a shot from a rifle hit him in the chest and passed entirely through, knocking him to the ground. Unable to fight on, Hill crawled to the rear of the stable out of the line of fire.

A shot through the top of the roof ricocheted into the coach taking a chunk of wood with it, and both projectiles struck messenger Smith in the forehead, knocking him senseless on the floor of the coach. Since Smith was bleeding profusely from the head wound, messenger Davis thought he was dead or dying. Davis returned fire as fast as he could reload. Finally he decided his best course of action would be to exit the coach door opposite the stable and make his way to a large pine tree across the road. He carefully kept the coach between him and the robbers as he retreated. Davis kept firing at the cracks in the logs as he backed across the road, hoping to keep the robbers' heads down and interfere with their aim. Campbell had decided to stay with Davis rather than be trapped in the coach and was following closely behind. The telegraph operator was unarmed and had no way of defending himself, so when he strayed to the left, he was wounded and went to his knees in the roadway. When all the robbers then opened up on the stationary target and riddled the unarmed man with bullets, Campbell fell over dead.

Davis made it to the tree and from this new place of cover continued the gunfight with the robbers. Davis called to Barnett, the stagecoach driver, to leave the coach and make a run for it or to take the coach out of the station, but before he could whip up the six-horse team, Frank McBride ran out and grabbed the leaders. Davis fired at the exposed robber, and McBride threw up his hands, fell over backwards, then crawled around behind the horses and got back into the stable. Charles Carey then came out using the coach for cover and ordered Barnett to come down off the boot. He placed the driver in front of him and advanced on Davis. The two men exchanged threats, but the messenger realized he could not shoot the robber without hitting Barnett. Relying on the safe to protect the treasure for an entire day and realizing that he needed help, he left the station and started on foot southward toward Beaver Creek. He planned to get the other three messengers and return.

Davis walked 7 miles to Ben Eager's ranch and borrowed a horse. He soon met Jesse Brown, Billy Sample, and Boone May on the road as they were heading north to see why the treasure coach had not arrived on schedule. The four messengers returned and found the robbers gone, the safe opened, and the treasure captured. The men learned that the robbers had rounded up all the men and tied them to trees, telling them that someone would be along at 10:00 P.M. to release them. They then spent only a few hours opening the safe. At 9:30 P.M., before the four messengers arrived, the stock tender managed to free himself from the grain room and untie the other captives before starting off for Deadwood to report the affair.

Hill was taken to the Cold Springs Ranch where Dr. F. L. Babcock of Deadwood treated his wounds. At first it was thought he would die; the arm wound was not serious, and the rifle bullet had passed through his body without striking a vital organ, so he fully recovered. Smith's wound was found to be only superficial.

Stagecoach robbery had been tolerated by most as little more than a nuisance, perhaps because most people were not affected by the crime, but murder was altogether another matter. With the entire countryside outraged, it was decided that the time had come to purge the Deadwood to Cheyenne Road of all highwaymen, and posses went out in all directions.

<> <> <>

A few weeks before the *Monitor* was jumped at Cañon Springs, Governor John W. Hoyt, Marshal William R. Schnitger, and Postmaster Herman Glafcke wrote to Washington asking for aid in stopping the mail robberies. The correspondence was accompanied by a comprehensive file of articles from the *Leader* representing the condition of affairs. As a result the Department of Justice authorized an expenditure of $2,000. These funds provided the opportunity to pay $5.00 a day to each man selected for posse duty. Colonel Adams of the Post Office Department was charged with organizing the Cheyenne party. He went to Cheyenne and was sworn in as a deputy U.S. marshal and then selected Scott Davis, Boone May, and eight other good men for his party. They went to Fort Laramie for horses, ammunition, and supplies and then headed north into the Inyan Kara country. Meanwhile Seth Bullock had organized another party from Deadwood and headed south along the stage route to Jenney's Stockade, then swung north again following a wagon trail toward Rapid City. On September 28, with several parties already in the field, Luke Vorhees, superintendent of the stage line, issued a proclamation of reward:

$2,500 reward. Will be paid for the return of the money and valuables and the capture (upon conviction), of the five men who robbed our coach on the 26th day of September, 1878 at Cañon Springs (Whiskey Gap) Wyo. Ter. of twenty-seven thousand dollars, consisting mostly of gold bullion. Pro rate of the above amount will be paid for the capture of either of the robbers and proportionate part of the property.

The commissioners of Laramie County engaged five men under the leadership of Ed Ordway and agreed to pay each man $5.00 per day. They took the field on Sunday, September 29. Nearly every day some new party was organized to follow a clue or a trail, each party hoping to collect a portion of the large reward offered by the stage line, the $200 per robber offered by the U.S. government, and the $200 per robber offered by the county's commissioners.

Immediately after leaving the Cañon Springs Station, the robbers took separate trails, except for Carey who remained with the wounded McBride. All five men headed east into the Dakota Territory and, as prearranged to divide the loot, met on Reynold's Prairie at the convergence of the two forks of Castle Creek in Pennington County, Dakota Territory. From there the road agents separated again, with Albert Speers heading southeast toward Nebraska and Thomas Jefferson "Duck" Goodale heading east toward his home in Atlantic, Iowa. Carey and McBride headed east toward Newton's Fork with Albert Gouch riding point. The fifth man, George "Big Nose" Parrott, disappeared into Albany County's population and remained mostly in Wyoming over the next several years.

Carey, McBride, and Gouch arrived the following day at Newton's Fork, where the two robbers traded their saddle horses and $250 for two ponies and a spring wagon. Carey threw the saddles in the bed and made McBride as comfortable as possible. They were next seen turning northeast near Rockerville, Dakota Territory, heading in the direction of Rapid City.

Meanwhile W. M. Ward, division superintendent for the stage line, with Uri Gillette, was out searching for the outlaws and cut the trail of Carey and McBride's wagon at Slate Creek. Ward and Gillette followed long enough to determine that the fugitives were heading toward Rapid City and then hurried ahead to assemble a posse. Ward and Gillette were joined by John Brennan, Ed Cook, Bill Steel, "Doc" Pierce, Frank Moulton, C. B. Stocking, Dr. Whitfield, Howard Worth, Peter Hammerquist, Emmet James, and several others who played out early and returned to town. Ward learned that the spring wagon had been seen the evening of the September 27 near Rockerville and would probably be at Rapid Creek the following day. The posse quickly moved down Rapid Valley but could find no trace of the fugitives.

McBride's wound had slowed the outlaws' progress, so that they crossed the path of the posse well after it had passed Mitchell Creek. When the posse was returning to Rapid City, it cut the trail of the wagon, but some of the men were already discouraged and exhausted and went home. Soon after finding the wagon tracks, Ward's posse was joined by Seth Bullock's party, but Bullock's men and horses were spent, so only a few men remained to reinforce Ward's diminished posse.

During the evening of September 29, the two posses camped near Mitchell Creek, and one member was sent out to reconnoiter the surrounding country. He discovered the fugitives' camp hidden in a small ravine near Pine Springs a short distance off the road. The horses had been turned out to graze, and three men were well settled, so the scout, believing he had not been observed, returned to his camp to report. The men discussed the situation and decided to make their attack upon the robbers' camp at daylight. As dawn broke, the posse surrounded the camp and found that "the birds had flown," leaving behind the wagon and a few supplies. The posse could find no tracks or were so exhausted and disappointed that they did not want to continue the pursuit. They decided that the fugitives had relentlessly pursued an easterly course so they gave up and returned to Rapid City, except Ward who continued east to Pierre.

Gouch, after the three fugitives realized they had been discovered, left the party and headed for Fort Thompson while Carey and McBride, to avoid the Rapid City posse, decided to head west, turning back into familiar Wyoming country. They rode throughout the early morning hours and were well away from their campsite by daybreak of September 30. They continued until they were back inside Wyoming and by October 2 had made their way to Jenney's Stockade, traveling only 50 miles in thirty-six hours. Near the stockade the two fugitives ran headlong into Scott Davis's party. Davis knew McBride on sight, having seen him holding the leaders at the stage station, and recognized the wound he had inflicted upon the robber. Carey, though well known, was also recognized from the scene of the robbery when he had used driver Barnett as a shield.

On October 3 one of the stage drivers, upon arriving at Deadwood, "confirmed the hanging of a road agent near Cañon Springs and says others will soon share the same fate." On October 9 Cheyenne's *Leader* reprinted a story from the *Deadwood Times*.

THE GOOD WORK PROGRESSES

Deputy Sheriff's Davis and Radcliff of Central, returned yesterday and reported that they found the bodies of two men hanging to a pine tree about seven miles from Jenny's Stockade, at a point four miles east of the road from the stockade to Custer. They were black in the face, with tongues and eyes protruding, and were a ghastly looking spectacle. Both wore the California riveted brown clothing and had light colored hair and moustache. They had been hanging for some time, and it is thought that the Scott Davis party did the good work last week. The sheriffs did not molest them, but left them to swing and fester in the sun, a warning to others of the same ilk.

None of the men in the Davis party ever confirmed that these two men were hanged by them or that they were Carey and McBride, and the deputies from Central were either too distant from the remains to comment further, or to identify two strangers who were so badly decomposed. However, the *Leader* provided a description of the two fugitives that coincided with the brief description of the two hanged men:

Two of the Cañon Springs stage robbers are described as follows: Charles Cary [sic], 27 years old, light complexion, brown hair; if any beard, little sandy; six feet high; has new, large Ulster overcoat, a little gray; carries a Winchester cartridge belt; pockmarks on each side of his nose . . . Frank McBride, who is supposed to be with Cary [sic], is a small man, with small features; small feet, light brown hair, light moustache and goatee; weighs 145 pounds; is 24 years old; very sharp eyes, supposed to be wounded . . .

Perhaps most convincing was that the grave of McBride was never found along the clear trail left by the two fugitives, and it was certain he was alive on September 30 when seen in camp near Pine Springs. He had sufficiently recovered to saddle-up and ride but still needed the services of a doctor for a serious though apparently not fatal stomach wound, and no doctor was ever contacted. Both men just seemed to disappear on about October 2 without a trace.

<> <> <>

Ward had gone on to Pierre when his party lost the fugitives at Pine Springs and expected to find some word of Carey and McBride, but instead he got a lead on Thomas Jefferson "Duck" Goodale of Atlantic, Iowa. He went to Goodale's hometown and, while walking down the street, saw on display in a bank's window the largest of the stolen gold bars marked "no. 12," which was worth $4,300. He inquired and from bank owner Almond Goodale learned that Almond's son had received the bullion as payment for a rich mining claim in Wyoming. He proudly displayed his son's good fortune. Ward had "Duck" Goodale arrested, and his father turned over the gold and other stolen items to authorities. Ward started for Cheyenne on the train with his prisoner.

Goodale escaped from the train on his way to Wyoming by going into the washroom alone and slipping his shackles. After the bands and chains were found on the floor, the train was backed a half mile to the place he had jumped off, but the search was futile. The *Leader* reported:

Duck Goodale, the road agent who escaped from Ward at Lone Tree, Neb. on Tuesday night, is thus described in the circular issued by the stage company: About 27 years old, 5 feet 11 inches high, and weighs about 180 pounds; has dark hair and when he escaped wore a thin beard of two week's growth.

The stage line offered a reward of $700 for his recapture and Laramie County added $200, but he was not heard of again. Ward was suspected of complicity in the escape and dismissed by the stage line.

Albert Speers, alias Davis, sold $800 in gold dust and $500 in jewelry in Ogallala, Nebraska. A detective in that city was suspicious and arrested Speers at Wood River as he was trying to sell more jewelry. Speers was returned to Wyoming and convicted of second-degree murder on November 28, 1878. He insisted that he had arrived late at Reynold's Prairie and received a short count on his share, and it seems he had been cheated as he could account for less than $2,000 of the plunder. Although he later said that some of the loot was buried at Wood

River, none was ever found, and he could give no directions to its location. He was tried, convicted, and sent to the penitentiary in Nebraska to serve his time. His sentence was commuted on April 26, 1886, and he received a full pardon, restoring all his civil rights, on September 24, 1889. In all he served ten years and ten months for his part in killing Campbell.

Andy Gouch was not prosecuted as an accessory-after-the-fact, and perhaps the decision not to prosecute him was a deal he made to lead authorities to hidden gold dust valued at $11,000 dollars. This would have been the shares of Carey and McBride and the larger amount, representative of Speers shortfall, may have been allowed because Carey was the leader and Speers was absent at the division. Of the $27,000 stolen, approximately three-fourths was recovered, and a small portion spent. The missing portion represented George Parrott's share, which included the gold bar valued at $2,000, some of the currency, and some gold dust. While Parrott was never arrested for, or conclusively implicated in, the Cañon Springs robbery, he died an ignominious death at the end of a lynch mob's rope on March 22, 1881.

CHAPTER TEN

A SHARP NEVADA ROAD AGENT

Milton A. Sharp and William C. Jones robbed stagecoaches in California and Nevada in 1880. When they stopped the Bodie to Carson City coach in Nevada on September 5 by killing one of the horses, legendary shotgun guard Mike Tovey shot and killed Jones. Tovey was wounded in the exchange and, after he was taken to a nearby farmhouse for treatment, Sharp returned to the coach and demanded Wells, Fargo's treasure box. Wells, Fargo & Company assigned their premier detective, James B. Hume, to the case. He exhumed Jones's body, found a San Francisco bank book, and traced it to a boarding house in that city. Within a few days Sharp was under arrest and extradited to Nevada for trial. He was sentenced to serve twenty years at Nevada's state prison, but reformed and was paroled after serving only fourteen years.

Milton Anthony Sharp's mother, Elisabeth, managed to raise her family of eight—four sons and four daughters—near Lee's Summit, Missouri, without the assistance of their father. She was determined that her children receive at least a moderate education. After Milton completed his schooling, he helped support the family until he left home in 1866, at the age of twenty-six. He made his way to California and Nevada where he worked as a miner over the next dozen years. In spite of his penchant for investing in questionable mining stocks (or because of it), he never managed to strike it rich. In 1879, after going broke once again, Milton was working on the farm of Peter Ahart on the outskirts of Auburn, California, when he met William C. Jones, alias Frank Dow. Jones had just been released from prison and took a menial job on the Ahart farm, but the ex-convict still had a desire to find the perfect opportunity to make a "big haul."

Sharp had been a good boy and had grown into a good, law-abiding man, but Jones managed to convince Sharp to join him in a stagecoach-robbing spree and assured his thirty-nine-year-old "green" partner that he had learned the business well. The two aspiring road agents worked at the Ahart farm for a while, accumulating a stake, and then disappeared. They stocked a deserted cabin and laid low for months, hoping they would be forgotten.

On May 15, 1880, the two men suddenly appeared on the road between Forest Hill, California, and Auburn Station, less than a mile away, and stopped the down coach. They made the passengers line up along the road, went through them and the driver, taking $150 dollars and several valuable watches. Then they quickly made their escape into Nevada.

On June 8 Jones and Sharp stopped the Carson City to Aurora coach driven by Silas Cambridge, carrying seven passengers, when it was in the vicinity of George Dalzell's Station between Sulphur Springs and Sweetwater. Aboard when the coach left Carson City were: Edward B. Shaw, Mr. Rowe, Mr. Kinssendorf, J. F. Nugent, Mrs. Cass, John O'Donnell, and S. Gambriner, but two of the men got off at some way station along the route. Both road agents were masked and held shotguns on the driver while they ordered him to throw out the treasure box. He complied immediately. The passengers who were still aboard were ordered out and told to line up and place their hands on their heads. One of the robbers held his shotgun on the passengers while the other went through them for valuables.

Nugent said that when the coach was stopped he took off his gold watch chain and a gold ring and put them in the hollow of his palm, saving them from the robbers; his silver watch and $14 dollars were collected. Shaw of Cutting & Company was relieved of a gold watch and chain and $12, but the robbers overlooked $100 in a side pocket. Mrs. Cass was robbed of $9—all she had—and Kinssendorf was forced to give up his lunch but saved $37 by dropping it between his pants and drawers. When Kinssendorf was asked if he had any money and answered that he had none, one of the robbers remarked he would give him a half dollar coin but never handed it over. They even searched the driver, taking his watch, but promised to return it "when next we meet."

The road agents delayed the coach for more than an hour while working on the express box and finally took out $3,000 before telling the driver to continue on his route. It was estimated that the aggregate take was over $4,000. The driver hurried into Aurora to report the robbery. Wells, Fargo's Carson City agent, H. L. Tickner, took a shotgun messenger and went to the scene to investigate as soon as he heard of the robbery, but they could find no trace or clue.

A week later, on June 15, the duo stopped the up-coach on the Carson City to Bodie run 18 miles beyond Wellington's Station near Dalzell's Station, the same place they stopped the coach on June 8. Cambridge was driving again and, just as they came to a bend in the road that required the driver to slow his team, passenger John Cameron, riding next to the driver, asked, "Wasn't the stage robbed somewhere along here?"

Cambridge answered, "This is the very spot," and in that moment the same two road agents stepped onto the road and covered the men with shotguns. The coach was stopped and the box thrown out when the order was given, but this time it carried only $300. The robbers did not molest the driver or Cameron, nor the inside passengers which included Mrs. R. Crown, Mrs. McBride and child, I. Stead, and I. W. Smith. An hour later the down-coach loaded with bullion passed the same location, but it passed the spot safely, probably because there were three shotgun messengers on board. The *Carson Daily Appeal* on June 17 had an opportunity to reflect on the frequency of the robberies on the Carson City to Bodie route:

ROBBERS BEHIND TIME

There was no attempt made yesterday to rob the Bodie stage. When the stage reached the spot where the robberies generally occur the horses stopped as usual and remained at a dead standstill for about fifteen minutes from force of habit. No robbers appeared, and then they jogged on. It is supposed that the footpads over slept themselves. The robbers who do business along the Bodie line should be up and stirring with the lark or else they are liable to get left. The stage from Carson is a fast concern and can't bother to wait for road agents who are not promptly on hand. Business is business with us every time.

On June 22 the *Appeal* remarked that they had recently published a "foot pad map" to guide parties in pursuing the road agents. Virginia City's *Territorial Enterprise* reported:

In the history of journalism in this country there has probably never been so marked an instance of appreciation of enterprise as that displayed by the entire press of the land for work performed by the Carson Appeal in publishing a map of the route taken by the Bodie stage robbers, for the guidance of Indians in pursuit of the highwaymen. It is true the Indians have not caught the robbers yet, but that is the fault of the Indians, not the map.

Jones and Sharp wrote to the editor of the *Appeal:*

Sweetwater, June 19, 1880

Editor Appeal: We pause a few moments on our route south to state that we have just received a copy of your map marking our movements since we robbed the Bodie stage. In our opinion your meddlesome interference is wholly without the province of journalism. The map is correct as far as it goes but it will never do the State any service. We have already ordered a fresh lot printed at the Bodie News office (never heard of the paper–Ed.) and when the Indians get hold of them they will be thrown completely off the scent. If in future you will devote yourself to the business of instructing the Republican party of Ormsby County and let our business take care of itself we have every reason to believe that your paper will give much better satisfaction in Nevada.

Yours,

Slim Jim

Club-Foot Jack

The standard $300 per robber reward had been posted by Wells, Fargo for the capture and conviction of the two road agents, so several posses were soon in the field. A large force of Indians was also pursuing the robbers and Wells, Fargo detective James B. Hume was brought out of Utah and put on the case. It was getting too hot for Jones and Sharp in Nevada. With several good hauls to split between them, they decided to lay low for a while and crossed over into California.

On August 6 the two masked road agents took up their positions a short distance from the Grizzly Bear House, 2 miles from Auburn. At 6:30 P.M. they "jumped" the up stage from Auburn to Forest Hill as it was climbing the North Fork Hill. They ordered the passengers to get out and line up, and one of the robbers held a shotgun on them while the second robber tried to open the treasure safe bolted inside the passenger compartment.

He could not get it open, so the robbers had the passengers board. The road agent ordered the driver to steer his team a quarter mile off the road. Once again they lined up the passengers and then managed to break the safe free from the coach. When it was on the ground, they opened the iron box with a hammer and cold chisel and found $1,500 inside. Next they went through the two passengers. From John McAllis they took $100, but he was able to drop his valuable gold watch into his boot. From Father Cassidy, a Catholic priest from Oakland, they took $80 and a gold watch valued at $250. The priest pleaded for them to return the watch, which had been given to him by friends, but they refused. The robbers then ordered the driver to return to the road and continue on his way, while they went off in a different direction. Silas Cambridge, who had also been driving the coach during their first heist, said later he was certain these were the same men.

<> <> <>

Jones and Sharp decided that things had cooled sufficiently in Nevada to return. On September 4 at 9:00 P.M., the two men stopped the Bodie to Carson City coach near the forks of Hall's and Simpson's Roads 9 miles south of Wellington's Station, but they were interrupted and fled without getting anything. At 2:30 A.M. the return coach was 5 miles from the place where the previous robberies had occurred. Shotgun guard Mike Tovey, who rode next to the driver, saw footprints in the roadway traveling in the same direction as the coach and ordered the driver to stop. He lit a lantern and got down to investigate, and then about every half mile he repeated the process. When they reached the place the coach had been stopped the night before, Tovey got down and, as before, bent over to examine the tracks next to the near leader of the team. Just then Jones and Sharp appeared out of the darkness and the first robber, Jones, covered Tovey with a rifle and ordered, "Throw up your hands, you ___."

Sharp was behind Jones and said, "You are trying to sneak up on us, are you?"

Tovey straightened up and, throwing up his hands, said, "Don't shoot; I'll go back and get the box."

Jones replied, "Go back, you whelp, and if you make a move we'll murder every mother's son of you." As Jones spoke, Sharp, also armed with a rifle, stepped around his partner and fired a single shot toward Tovey, but the bullet went into the chest of the near leader. The horse

M. A. Sharp
WELLS FARGO BANK, N.A.

lunged forward several times and then sank to the ground, dead. The others horses began to lunge and rear, but they could not run away because the dead horse held them in place.

This distracted the robbers long enough for Tovey to make his way behind the stagecoach. He was now behind the lamps, so that he was in darkness while both robbers were at the dim edge of the light from the coach lamps. Tovey whispered to J. Billings, the division agent who was also riding guard on the box, "Hand down that gun," and Billings passed down Tovey's double-barreled shotgun. Tovey crouched behind the coach and rested the barrel of his shotgun on the rear wheel, then waited patiently for the robbers to advance on the coach. Sharp moved to the right to flank the coach while Jones came straight forward saying, "Don't move or I'll murder every last . . ."

Tovey shouted out, "Who's moving?" which covered the sound of cocking his shotgun. Tovey then continued in a tone simulating fear, "You've got the drop on us. Come and get what you want." Tovey's voice must have convinced Jones that he had the upper hand because he lowered his rifle and advanced into the full glare of the lamps. Tovey then said loudly to the driver, "Throw down the box, quick, and let's get out of this."

Jones, muttering more about murdering everybody, moved forward again until he was next to the fallen leader and said, "Your heads are level." These were the last words he spoke as Tovey opened up with the right barrel of his shotgun, and the load of heavy buckshot took effect in the robber's face, killing him instantly. The dead man fell under the horses, and one of the swingers, a middle horse in a six-up, began to rear and lunge, stomping Jones's legs to mush.

Within a few seconds Billings had retrieved his weapon and fired several rounds at Sharp while Tom Woodruff, the messenger riding inside the coach, pulled his six-shooter and also fired at the second robber. Sharp was returning fire when Tovey ran to the rear of the coach and came face to face with Sharp not 20 yards away. Tovey fired one barrel, but without effect. The road agent returned fire striking Tovey in the right arm, shattering one of the bones between the wrist and elbow. Tovey dropped his shotgun causing the second barrel, which he had reloaded after shooting Jones, to discharge. Tovey next managed to pull his revolver with his left hand and fire after the fleeing robber twice, but, since he was right handed, his shots missed. Tovey examined his wound and saw that he was bleeding profusely, so he called to Billings and Woodruff to take him to Hall and Simpson's house not far off the road. Woodruff, who had pursued Sharp into a stand of willows but lost him there, returned. He and Billings then took Tovey to the farmhouse where the bleeding was stopped and the wound bandaged.

As soon as the three guards were out of sight, the driver heard a voice say, "Throw down that box," and he looked back to find Sharp covering him with a Henry rifle. The driver, who was unarmed, threw down the box and Sharp cut it open with a hatchet. He pocketed the few hundred dollars it held but in his haste missed a package of $800 in coins. The robber next asked the driver which way his partner had gone, as Sharp was behind the stage and could not see Jones lying in the road between the horses. The driver, who was afraid to speak the truth, said he did not know. Sharp walked off into the darkness, calling to his partner several times as he made his way into the brush.

The messengers came back in a short time and were surprised to hear that the road agent had been so brazen as to come back after the treasure. The guards examined the dead robber and saw that the buckshot had struck him in the lower part of his face, taking out the lower jaw; one buckshot had also taken out an eye, and there was blood oozing from several neck wounds. The deceased was tall, dark of complexion, with a black moustache and probably a goatee, as there were some remnants of a beard on the lower part of the neck that remained. The deceased was dressed in dark clothes, but there seemed little else to determine his identity. The dead man was carried a short distance off the road and buried deep enough to protect it from scavengers, and the grave was marked so it could easily be found later.

Detective Hume was still investigating the series of stagecoach robberies, so he went to the scene and exhumed the dead robber's remains. He returned to Carson City on September 10 and told the editor of the *Daily Appeal* that he had cleaned up the face of the corpse and took a long look, but could not identify the remains though he had expected to recognize him as a man who worked the roads in lower California. He had gone through the deceased's pockets for clues and collected the mask he wore, which was made of black glazed oilcloth of the type used in carriage tops. Hume then left for California on the next stagecoach.

From a bank deposit book he found in the dead robber's pocket, which he kept secret from the editor of the *Appeal*, he learned that the

Mike Tovey
WELLS FARGO BANK, N.A.

two men shared a room in a Minna Street boarding house in San Francisco. The book also showed that both men had made substantial deposits in the Savings Union on the same day, and that the deceased robber was named W. C. Jones, and the fugitive was M. A. Sharp.

Hume coordinated his efforts with the police in San Francisco. The chief of police detailed detectives to examine the fugitives' room and two of his men found, in a valise, the watch and chain belonging to E. B. Shaw, another stolen watch and ring, and material resembling the dead robber's mask. The two detectives remained in the room waiting for Sharp to return, and finally he arrived telling the landlady he had come for his valise. The officers sprang from the room and covered Sharp with pistols, threw their prisoner to the floor, took a new Colt's six-shooter from his belt, and put on the handcuffs. Their prisoner had been carrying a roll of blankets that contained another six-shooter and a bowie knife, which the officers collected. Sharp was then searched thoroughly, and the detectives found $1,600 in a money belt tied around his waist and $800 sewn into his coat lining. Sharp gave his correct name but denied knowing anyone named W. C. Jones. He said he had only come to get his property to move to another house and claimed a partner named Frank Keith but could not say where he was. The landlady was then given the description of Jones, and she confirmed that Jones was the man who shared the room with Sharp.

Hume took custody of the prisoner and returned him to Carson City on September 18. By October 1 the prisoner was lodged in the Aurora jail with his bail set at $10,000. The grand jury had returned seven indictments: four for robbery of Wells, Fargo & Company, one for robbing driver Cambridge, one for robbing Ed Shaw, and one for attempting to kill Mike Tovey.

On October 24 Sharp escaped from the jail by making a hole in the east side of the courthouse through a wall three bricks thick. The streets were crowded, so a large posse was soon raised and began scouring the hills. He was soon captured and his trial, set for October 27, was not delayed. He had been indicted on numerous counts but on October 30 was only convicted on the second indictment for robbery. Trial on indictments three through seven were postponed. Sharp was sentenced to twenty years in prison on the first conviction for robbery, so all the other charges were dropped. On November 12 Sharp was delivered to the Nevada State Prison, where he was registered as prisoner no. 158.

Sharp, through model behavior, earned trusty status, which gave him the opportunity to escape from prison, which he did on August 15,

1889. Sharp remained free for several years, taking work at menial jobs in California to remain unnoticed. On the evening of June 15, 1893, Mike Tovey was shot and killed while riding messenger on the Ione to Jackson stagecoach. The robber made no effort to rob the stage after the killing, raising strong suspicion that it had been a murder for revenge committed by Sharp. This renewed the effort to find the escapee, and on September 28, 1893, he was recognized and arrested. Sharp gave a detailed account of his whereabouts for the years after he escaped from prison and, consequently, was cleared of the murder of Tovey. Sharp was returned to the Nevada State Prison but was paroled, on the recommendation of Hume and other influential men, on July 10, 1894.

CHAPTER ELEVEN

A TEXAS BAD MAN IN COLORADO

Hamilton White, alias Henry Burton, robbed stagecoaches single-handedly in Texas using a peculiar disguise. He moved his one man operation to Arkansas in 1881 and began using a bright lamp to blind the driver and passengers before they were hooded and tied. White always gave the impression that there were several more road agents just out of sight in the shadows. He moved on to Colorado, authorities close on his trail, and when he lit up the Alamosa coach he was arrested within hours. He soon found himself convicted and serving a federal sentence in Wyoming's prison at Laramie.

Hamilton "Ham" White, an only child born in 1853, lived in Cedar Creek, Bastrop County, Texas, with his mother and father. In 1873 his father was murdered and Ham was certain he knew the killer. He avenged his father's death under circumstances that led to his indictment for murder in 1876. Facing trial, Ham had to fund his defense, so he robbed a mail coach but, because of his inexperience, failed to disguise himself and was soon identified and arrested. Following a brief trial for mail robbery in the circuit court, he was convicted and sentenced to a term at the penitentiary in West Virginia, which contracted with the U.S. government to hold federal prisoners. In December 1880

President Rutherford B. Hayes granted White a pardon and the twenty-seven-year-old man returned home. By that time, however, White had suffered a number of serious injuries—he was blind in one eye, had a right "cork leg," and a bone in his right arm had been removed.

White had hardly settled on the family farm when he learned that his indictment for murder was still pending and he would again be required to post bond to remain free. Now, with prospects leaner than in 1876, he returned to the road again to finance his defense. In February 1881 he robbed a mail coach on the San Antonio to Austin line not 50 miles from the capital, but this time he used the knowledge he gained in prison and donned a peculiar disguise. There was not enough evidence to focus suspicion on him then, but when two more mail coaches were robbed—by the same footpad in the same peculiar disguise—and at the same location, attention turned to the convicted road agent. Realizing that it was only a matter of time before he again faced arrest for mail robbery and another lengthy prison term, Ham used his defense fund to flee from Texas.

White assumed the alias Henry W. Burton. He traveled to Fayetteville, Arkansas, in late May and on June 4 left that city for Alma, searching for an opportunity. On June 15 the mail coach between Alma and Fayetteville was robbed by a lone, carefully disguised highwayman using an unusual *modus operandi* by blocking the road and shining a bright light on the stagecoach to blind the driver and passengers. The road agent stole a distinctive watch with a silver case and heavy gold-plated chain from H. S. Gray, along with about $100 in currency from the passengers. Since the Arkansas officers were slow to make a case against Burton, he robbed another stagecoach in the meantime, but finally on June 24 the Arkansas authorities sent out descriptive circulars by telegraph and posted a $400 reward for Burton's capture. In the circular Burton was described as 5 feet 10 inches in height, weight about 165 pounds with a light complexion, sandy hair and moustache, blue or gray eyes, hands white with long fingers, and lame in his right leg.

Burton had already fled from Arkansas by the time the authorities began their pursuit. The fugitive passed through Pierce City, Missouri, and arrived at Pueblo, Colorado, on June 19. By the time the authorities showed up, however, all sign of him was lost, so the Arkansas lawmen returned home and waited. Burton had continued on to Alpine, then Pitkin, on to Gunnison, and finally arrived at Lake City on June 26. He had again been looking for an opportunity and found it in the mail coach running between Lake City and Alamosa.

He went to Alamosa, Colorado, on June 27 and hired a horse from the livery, paying a guarantee of $150 to ensure its return. He had already traveled the stagecoach route in coming to Alamosa and had selected a remote site for the robbery 11 miles west of town, where he had cached his supplies. He rode to the spot and began preparations for the arrival of the coach. He stretched a pole across the road to stop the horses and then strung a canvas curtain from a tree so that it covered him down to his waist. He cut a dozen hoods from woolen material, cut holes, and threaded string so they could be tied in place. Next he pulled out a new oil reflector lamp and prepared it for use.

A little after midnight on June 28, the mail coach arrived with F. B. Cutler seated on the roof behind the driver. Cutler later said that he saw in the distance a dim light, but thought it was from a teamster's camp some distance off the road. He then looked on the road ahead and saw that there was a pole placed across the path of the horses and told the driver of the obstruction just as the coach stopped. The driver said, "Hell is to pay here," when a voice called out, "Drive up a little further."

Since the driver saw that a man covered him with a pistol, he did as he was told and was then instructed to drive a little further again. Once the coach was in the exact position satisfactory to the robber, it came under a strong light from the reflector, which had been positioned behind the canvas curtain and was the source of the "dim" light first seen. The bright, focused light momentarily blinded the men on the outside of the coach.

Burton made every effort to make it seem as if there were several confederates in his party and announced, "No one will get hurt if you do not shoot. Get down on this side of the coach. If you get down on the other side you will be shot." The driver objected, saying, "I cannot let go of this team, they will run away," but Burton, depending on the pole to hold the team, said that another man was then holding the reins.

There were four men on top, including the driver, and eight men and one woman inside, for a total of thirteen aboard. The men on top came down one at a time, were hooded, and ordered to kneel in the road with their hands on their heads. The inside passengers were then ordered out one at a time, ordered to kneel, and hooded. Most of the men then had their hands tied behind them. The woman was neither hooded nor tied. Once the situation was entirely under Burton's control he warned the men, "Don't you lift those caps at the risk of your lives," and then searched the men for their valuables, finding in all about $1,000 and a pistol. Burton next threw out the mailbags and asked the driver for the express box and pouches, but there were none. He cut open the mailbags while the woman was required to hold the light. He moved the registered packages a short distance from the coach and ripped them apart, taking everything of value, including a bag of ore addressed by John Strom to assayer Eugene E. Burlingame at Post Office Box 2555. When this was completed, he left so suddenly and quietly that the men remained kneeling several minutes before they realized the robber had departed.

The men were untied, removed their hoods, and then gathered up the damaged mail, missing the registered packages because they were some distance from the coach. They threw the damaged mail sacks into the coach. Passenger J. P. McMillan, who had also been seated on top next to the driver, collected the reflector lamp and kept his hood as a souvenir. The passengers hurriedly climbed aboard while the driver removed the pole blocking his team, and the coach sped into Alamosa to report the holdup.

Burton, who had a good start on the coach, arrived in town an hour before the alarm was sounded. He had returned his horse to the stable and collected his deposit before he boarded the train to Pueblo, accompanied by many of the victims of his late night raid on the coach. During breakfast at Placer, Burton was regaled by stories of the thrilling robbery. On the same train with Burton was Deputy Postal Inspector L. Cass Carpenter, but the description of the Arkansas road agent he had received said the fugitive was elderly. He had no information on the Alamosa stagecoach bandit, so, while he was suspicious of Burton and pondered his next move, he was distracted and his man disappeared.

◇ ◇ ◇

On June 29 at 2:00 P.M., the train reached Pueblo, where City Marshal Patrick G. Desmond found Burton standing on the platform leaning against the ticket office window. He arrested Burton based on the Arkansas circular, and Burton insisted that Desmond must be mistaken. When the prisoner was searched at the jail, he had in his possession $478, the watch taken in the Arkansas robbery, and the pistol and bag of ore from the Alamosa robbery. Desmond telegraphed that he had the Alamosa stagecoach robber and was told to bring the prisoner to Denver as soon as it was practical, and the city marshal immediately made arrangements.

When Burton was taken from his cell in Pueblo's jail and hand-cuffed, he offered Desmond $500 to let him escape. He said he would go to his home in West Virginia to get more money and then return to stand trial. Desmond refused, and the trip to Denver on the Rio Grande train began. The doors of the train were left open to take advantage of a cool breeze flowing through the car as the train moved ahead at full speed. Desmond went to get a drink of water and glanced back just in time to see his prisoner making for the door with Desmond's small valise. Burton, because of his game leg, could not run as fast as Desmond so the marshal caught up with Burton and grabbed his shoulder when he was on the car's rear platform, pulling him back toward the train; however, the prisoner still managed to jump to the road bed. The marshal then fired several shots after the fugitive, one grazing the bone behind

Burton's right ear. The lawman called out for someone to pull the bell cord. By the time the train stopped, Burton had managed to run 500 yards from the rails and had released one wrist from the cuffs.

Joined by several passengers in pursuing the escapee, Desmond, along with passenger Ed S. Keith, fired a volley of shots after the fleeing man. Burton searched the valise, expecting to find a pistol. When he found nothing with which to defend himself, he fell to the ground to avoid being shot. He said later that he had thought he would arise and continue running after the men exhausted their ammunition, but Desmond was too quick and came upon his prisoner while he was still lying down. The marshal replaced the cuffs, returned the prisoner to the train, and they continued on their way. After traveling some distance past Castle Rock, Burton again tried to escape by jumping through an open window, but Desmond, who had once again seemed distracted, was alert enough to get a firm grip on his prisoner and thwart his second escape attempt. Burton's attempts to flee seemed to strongly contradict his claim of innocence.

At 9:00 P.M. on July 1, Burton was taken before a U.S. Commissioner who said, "I understand, Mr. Burton, that you are charged with having committed a highway robbery on June 27, between Alamosa and Lake City in that you stopped a stagecoach and jeopardized the life of the driver with deadly weapons. Have you any counsel?"

The defendant said he did not have an attorney and then pled not guilty. Burton was asked if he could give bail. He said he could not, so the judge said, "Well, as this is a case of a good deal of importance I will have to hold you at $5,000," to which the prisoner only nodded. In a few minutes it was decided to hold the examination within the week, and the prisoner was remanded to the custody of a deputy U.S. Marshal, who lodged him in the county jail. While the defendant awaited his next court date, counsel was appointed by the court so he would have time to discuss the particulars of the defense with his client.

Burton's examination was held on July 8. After a heated exchange between the court appointed defense counsel and Pueblo City Marshal

Desmond, the lawman revealed that $470 of the stolen money was in the safe at Charpiot's Hotel. He also said that before he realized that the money in the prisoner's possession might be stolen property, the prisoner had spent $8 treating Pueblo's jail inmates.

The woolen mask and the reflector lamp were produced and identified by J. P. McMillan. Then the bag of ore and pistol, found on Burton when arrested, were offered into evidence and identified as items stolen during the Alamosa stagecoach robbery. Postmaster T. M. Finley had gone to the scene of the robbery, found the registered packages that had been mutilated by the robber, collected them, and sent them in care of the U.S. Circuit Court in Denver. He estimated that about $165 dollars had been stolen from the mails. The last bit of evidence was the prisoner's offer to pay Desmond $500 to let him escape and the details of his two attempts to flee from the train, a showing of guilty knowledge. The prisoner was held on $3,000 bail to await trial, which was held at the fall term of the circuit court in Colorado Springs, Colorado. The same evidence previously produced resulted in a guilty verdict. He was sentenced to life imprisonment in the penitentiary built at Laramie, Wyoming.

<> <> <>

Deputy U.S. Marshal Sim Cantril was responsible for delivering Burton to the Wyoming prison, and he also had Charles B. Dingman, another stagecoach robber, to deliver as well. He went to the county jail in Pueblo and waited in the office with chains while jailer Sam Drake went upstairs to open the cell door. There was nowhere for Burton to go but down to the office, so the jailer let him go alone. A chair was positioned for the prisoner to be seated while being chained, but as soon as Burton got into the office he pulled out what appeared to be a pistol, flashed it close to Cantril's face, and then pressed it hard against the lawman's breast. Burton told Cantril "throw up your hands," and then tried to reach around to take the pistol from Cantril's back hip pocket. The marshal's

Territorial Prison, Wyoming
WYOMING STATE ARCHIVES, DEPARTMENT OF STATE PARKS AND CULTURAL RESOURCES

pistol, however, was secured in his pocket in some manner that Burton could not overcome. As the prisoner struggled to free it, Cantril jumped back and was about to strike Burton with the chains, so the prisoner also jumped backward to avoid the blow. When the distance between the two antagonists gave Cantril the chance to draw his pistol, Burton immediately took a seat, surrendered, and handed over his weapon, which proved to be a dummy.

Burton's gun was a hard piece of leather, carefully worked to the shape of a .45 caliber pistol, with a hole bored in one end to look like the barrel. It had been wrapped in foil removed from cigarette packs, which made it appear nickel plated. He confessed that he had made the fake sometime earlier and had it hidden on his person for quite some time, awaiting the perfect moment to make his escape. He said he had taken careful note of the schedule of the trolley car and planned to use the weapon to "flesh" the officer while taking his gun, and then lock him inside the jail. He would next run out and take the trolley car's horse. Burton said that, now armed with a real revolver, he expected no resistance from the conductor and passengers and anticipated he would have at least a twenty-minute head start to put some distance between himself and the posse that would surely follow.

Cantril asked Burton if he would have used the lawman's gun. Burton replied that if he had been killed by the marshal he should not have cared because, being sentenced to prison for life, he cared nothing for his own existence. If he had to take a life to escape, he would have done so. He said that not one person in a thousand would have shown the courage and presence of mind exhibited by the marshal. He was securely chained and taken to Denver. The next morning, with nineteen-year-old Dingman, he was taken by train to the prison at Laramie. Burton arrived at the prison on October 7, 1881.

Burton was too desperate to serve time at a prison that had only wooden fences around its yard to secure him, so he was sent to the prison in Albany, New York. In 1886 he filed a writ of *habeas corpus* based upon trial error and was released on January 20, 1887. Burton went west and robbed stagecoaches in Texas before moving on to Arizona and California using the alias Henry Miller. He was caught and served time at Arizona's Territorial Prison in Yuma and California's San Quentin Prison, where he contracted tuberculosis. He was released on December 26, 1897, and returned to Texas. Next, he failed at two attempts to rob a train, and then tried extortion of a railroad and highway robbery, but without success. He died of tuberculosis on December 27, 1900, while in prison in his home state.

CHAPTER TWELVE

A LYNCHIN' BEE

When the stagecoach was robbed near Riverside, Arizona, on August 10, 1883, a posse was soon on the trail of the bandits. The lawmen captured one robber and two accessories. Two of these prisoners were lynched at Florence. Sheriff Bob Paul kept on the trail of the other two robbers and killed them in two harrowing shootouts in early October. The last accessory, a young man who had witnessed the lynching at Florence, died of fright two months after making bail. This was a rare case in which none of the stolen treasure was recovered.

Jack Almer's red hair and pale complexion made him look younger than his years and earned him the moniker "Red" Jack. His partners, relying on his disarmingly youthful appearance, sent Almer into Florence, Pinal County, Arizona Territory, in early August 1883 to reconnoiter Wells, Fargo & Company's operations. He sold his horses and left his saddle at the livery. You couldn't depend on Almer to be any particular place at any given time, except at the usual hour when the treasure box was loaded onto the Globe stagecoach, when he would be perched in view of the office. Because of this peculiar behavior, he was looked upon as a hard character, but, when nothing of note transpired for over a week, he was watched only casually. On Friday, August 10, Almer saw that it took two men to load the heavy treasure box into the driver's boot. He paid his passage as far as Riverside, saying he had to go there to obtain work in the mines, and then asked driver Humphrey to pick him up at the livery on his way out of town. Almer gathered his gear and, when the stagecoach pulled to a stop, put his saddle and bridle on the roof, climbed on top, and settled in behind the driver and messenger Johnny Collins. He pulled a bright red bandana from his pocket and tied it around his neck.

Meanwhile Joe Tuttle and Charles Hensley had established a camp in the mountains near Riverside where they could watch the road and see who was aboard the stage. They were seen Friday afternoon near the road in the large wash near the stagecoach station. They were loitering under a large mesquite tree, one of them sitting and the other lying down. Against the tree leaned their rifle and shotgun with their horses picketed near by.

When the stage passed by this point, Almer, concerned that his partners might not be able to see the red bandana, commenced loudly singing a ribald cowboy song. His presence on the stage was the signal that the treasure box was full. As soon as the stage passed, Tuttle and Hensley mounted and followed at a distance until twilight. They were only a few yards behind the stage when the driver pulled up at Evans & Le Blanc's Stage Station. The robbers made a careful survey of the coach to make certain that Almer had been aboard, as he would remain at the station, and then rode a short distance before turning off the road and heading towards the river. They rode along the riverbank to avoid being seen at Riverside. When they reached the ford 100 yards above Riverside station, they crossed over and rode on for 1½ miles to the point they had selected at the foot of the hill leading out of the Gila Valley. They had prepared the place sometime during the previous week by carefully tying back the branches of two bushes to give each robber full command of the road without exposing himself to view.

It was only a short wait until the stage passed between them, and they opened fire on the messenger and driver without a single word of warning. The messenger, Collins, was immediately killed from a charge of buckshot entering his chin and neck, but the robbers continued shooting until Humphrey called out, "For God's sake, stop shooting! You have killed one man. What more do you want?"

Next they shot dead one of the leaders and one of the wheelers, after which they ceased firing and proceeded to examine the stage. They discovered Felix Le Blanc alone inside the coach and ordered him to step out and drop his money onto the road. As soon as Le Blanc obeyed this command, they ordered him to throw out the express box, which was in the boot. He made an effort to do so; however, the box was very heavy and the dead messenger was lying on top of it. Seeing that Le Blanc could not remove the box alone, the robbers ordered Humphrey to drop the reins and assist him. The driver asked permission to remove the body of the murdered man from the boot, but was told, "Let him lie where he is and get that box out at once or we'll put holes through you s___s of b___s."

By almost superhuman effort the two men dragged the box from the boot and threw it onto the ground. The robbers next handed Le Blanc a new hatchet and ordered him to break open the box. As soon he had accomplished that work, they ordered both Le Blanc and Humphrey to march up the road in the direction of Cane Springs and accompanied the order with a threat of assassination should they attempt to return. The robbers took from the box $2,000 in silver and $500 in gold, hurriedly packed it into a single bundle, and strapped it onto one of the two remaining stage horses. They left $620 in currency in the box, having overlooked it in their haste. They also dropped, where their horses were hitched, a pair of leather saddlebags, a belt full of Winchester cartridges, a package of tea, a loaf of bread, and a distinctive handmade dirk knife.

Le Blanc and Humphrey continued up the road until they met the down stage at Cane Springs, about 3 miles from the scene of the robbery. There were several passengers aboard, with B. McKenny driving. McKenny and the passengers voted to camp at Cane Springs until daylight. To make sure that they would be safe, they climbed up the side of the mountain some distance above the road. At daylight they hitched up

Bob Paul (left, front) on the steps of the Pima County Courthouse
Arizona Historical Society, Tucson

and drove to the scene of the murder. The dead messenger was still lying on the boot face down and his gun was laying in the road a few steps in the rear of the stage, where it had dropped from his lap when the fatal charge of buckshot struck him. McKenny turned over the broken express box and found under it the $12 the robbers had made Le Blanc drop on the ground. They unharnessed the live horse and tied it onto the back of the down stage before proceeding into Riverside.

After accomplishing their work, the robbers took a trail circling to the right from the scene of the robbery and rode over the hills to the San

Pedro Road, reaching it at a point about 2 miles above Riverside. When they came to the road they stopped, and foot tracks indicated that they dismounted to divide the treasure into two packs so they could strap them more securely and evenly onto the stage horse. Here they dropped a nickel-plated no. 12 Winchester shotgun shell. From there the road agents followed the San Pedro Road and passed Dudleyville at a full gallop, one leading the pack horse and the other riding behind and whipping up the exhausted animal. Each man held a revolver in his right hand and both men were as silent as a tomb. The boys in front of the Dudleyville store hallooed to them and demanded the reason for their hurry, but they made no reply.

Five miles above Dudleyville, the robbers turned out of the road into the timber. Their tracks could not be followed because the ground was covered with a thick growth of summer grass. They killed the stage horse in the timber and buried the money, for when the robbers passed Mesaville 5 miles further on, they did not have the pack animal or packs with them. At 5:00 A.M. Saturday the robbers passed the Perdues' place where they were noticed by both Mrs. Perdue and Mrs. Pearson, who was a guest at the house. They were still riding at a high rate of speed and heading in the direction of Len Redfield's ranch.

The news of the robbery did not reach Florence until 10 A.M. Saturday. When Sheriff Andrew Doran was reached by telegraph in Pinal, he responded that he would meet the posse at Riverside. Undersheriff Lou Scanland and Fred Adams left for the scene and took the track of the fugitives, with orders to follow it as long as a trace remained. In the meantime J. P. Gabriel learned that "Red" Jack Almer had left the stage at Evans & Le Blanc's Stage Station and inquired if a horse had been left for him. When there was none, he had raved about treachery and asserted that he would make it "warm for them if they should fail to keep their agreement." Gabriel learned that Jack had brought with him a saddle and bridle but that he had started up the river on foot, leaving the saddle at the station but taking the bridle. Convinced by these facts that Almer was a party to the robbery, Gabriel decided to capture him.

A. J. Doran, Sheriff
ARIZONA HISTORICAL SOCIETY, TUCSON

The editor of the *Enterprise* joined Gabriel on the expedition, and they went to Putnam's corral to secure a horse and arms. Sheriff Doran was there, who had just returned from inspecting the robber's camp in the mountains. Doran took charge and saddled his animal, and the posse started at 10:00 A.M. Saturday in the direction of the San Pedro. Some time after midnight they reached Dudleyville and learned that Almer had given one of Mr. Finch's sons $15 to take him up river to Captain Cage's ranch, and that he had said to the boy during the journey that he must reach Redfield's that night. The posse borrowed two Winchester rifles and a six-shooter from Alex L. Pam of the Dudleyville store and pushed on. Just before daylight Sunday the posse arrived at Mesaville where they found Scanland, Adams, and Harrington, who had spent the night there. The three men came out from under their blankets promptly, saddled their horses, and joined Doran's posse. The posse arrived at the ranch of Woods & Brown in time for breakfast and secured fresh horses before pushing on to Captain Cage's ranch. There they learned that Almer had paid a young man named Huntley $10 to take him on to Redfield's.

The posse obtained fresh horses from G. M. Williams and by noon arrived at Frank Shield's place, where they found Frank Bernard in charge. While the posse ate and fresh horses were being saddled. Huntley came in and said that he was taking Almer to Redfield's when Frank Carpenter met them on the trail about ½ mile up. Carpenter and Almer dismounted and had a confidential talk, after which Carpenter gave Almer $10 with which to pay Huntley. Carpenter gave up his horse to Almer and walked down to Mesaville, and Almer rode on to Redfield's ranch alone.

With this new intelligence, the posse divided—three on each side of the river—and pushed on to Redfield's. They reached the ranch at 7:00 P.M. Sunday and swooped down upon the occupants unexpectedly. Joe Tuttle and Len Redfield were in sight with three other suspicious-looking strangers camped in front of the house, but they soon learned that Almer had passed through at 1:00 P.M. The posse anticipated a lively fight at this ranch but were disappointed and found Tuttle and Redfield meek as doves. The posse went into camp, keeping guard throughout the night to see that the "birds did not take wing" or ambush them. The next morning Sheriff Doran arrested Tuttle and Redfield and then made a careful search of the premises. He found a number of suspicious articles, including a U.S. mail sack. After the arrests it was decided that Gabriel would continue the pursuit of Almer while the rest of the party would return to Florence with the prisoners.

They found Frank Carpenter at Mesaville and arrested him. Scanland had on his saddle the saddlebags found at the scene of the robbery and, as soon as Carpenter saw them, he turned to Len Redfield and said, "Len, these fellows have got your saddlebags."

"Shut up!" was all that Redfield could say.

Investigation revealed that Tuttle was one of the robbers while Len Redfield and Frank Carpenter were accessories. The other principals, Almer and Charles Hensley, were well known. The robbers and their accessories were believed to be part of an organized gang of criminals who made their headquarters at Redfield's. Tucson's *Citizen* reported that:

For years Redfield's place had been a rendezvous for horse thieves and robbers who could always go there and get fresh horses and leave their old and broken down ones in place of them, or secrete their booty. There are men in Benson who saw Curly Bill [Brocius] at Redfield's when he was plying his vocation in and about Tombstone, also men who saw Murphy and Gibson there last spring. Parties in this town told the Redfields more than two years ago that they were harboring thieves and robbers; that their neighbors both above and below them thought hard of them and that they had better rid themselves of such men, or they would get into trouble. They did not thank the men who gave him [sic] this advice, and as good as told them that they had better attend to their own business.

The governor issued a reward proclamation:

GOVERNOR'S REWARD
*Whereas, Stage robbing is becoming apparently
a permanent industry of the Territory and
is one which carries with it the destruction of life and
always is attended with danger to
the peaceful traveling public, and
Whereas . . . highwaymen did stop
the coach on the Florence road,*

killing W. F. & Co.'s messenger, and
wounding the driver of said coach,
Now therefore, I, H. M. Van Arman,
Acting-Governor of the Territory of Arizona,
by virtue of the power vested in me,
do hereby offer a reward . . .
For the arrest and conviction of
the murderers on the Florence road,
ONE THOUSAND DOLLARS
Should fatal consequences to the robbers
attend their capture, identification and proof
that they were guilty parties will be sufficient
to secure the payment of the reward offered.
Done at the City of Prescott, the Capital,
the 13th day of August, A.D., 1883.

H. M. Van Arman
Acting Governor
Attest: John S. Furman
Assistant-Secretary
Arizona Territory

In addition to the "dead or alive" reward offered by the territory, Pinal County offered $200 and Wells, Fargo & Company had a standing reward of $300 for each robber, though these additional rewards were for arrest and conviction. This brought the total reward for each robber to $1,500.

Joe Tuttle provided two confessions, and each confession implicated the principals and the accessories. He insisted that he had only fired one shot while Hensley had fired seven times. Tuttle also said that the robbery was first proposed to him by Hensley and Almer in Johnsonville. The preliminary hearing was scheduled for Monday, August 27, and the defendants were held to answer and remanded to the sheriff, who lodged them in the county jail.

The following Monday morning Deputy U.S. Marshal Joseph Wiley Evans, accompanied by a posse of seven men, arrived at Florence with a writ of *habeas corpus* for Len G. Redfield. The town's people had been informed that among the posse was a close friend of Len Redfield named Bullis and Len's brother, Hank. The writ, issued by Judge Daniel Pinney, had been based upon affidavits setting forth that the life of Len Redfield was in danger from mob violence. As soon as Evans arrived, he served the writ on Undersheriff Scanland and placed his guards around the jail. Evans had planned to smuggle the prisoner out of town before dawn, but Scanland asked that Redfield be kept there until 7:00 A.M. to give him an opportunity to telegraph Sheriff Doran for instructions, and Evans agreed.

District Attorney Jesse Hardesty discovered Evans's guards at the jail and immediately protested against the procedure. Scanland then informed Evans that his guards must be withdrawn, as a deputy U.S. marshal had no authority to guard a county jail. Evans withdrew his guards. Hardesty next telegraphed Judge Pinney asking him to suspend his order. He also informed the judge that the town was arming and that any attempt to remove Redfield from the jurisdiction of the sheriff could result in his lynching, but the judge did not reply.

Once Evans's presence and purpose became known, the alarm was sounded, and the citizens, aroused to the highest pitch of indignation, assembled. The presence of Len's brother and a friend "armed to the teeth" gave the impression that the posse would, at the first opportunity, overpower Evans and set Redfield free. It was finally determined, after much debate, that Len Redfield should not be permitted to leave the town alive. Evans attempted to counter the rising bitterness by sending Hank Redfield and Bullis back to Tucson and by announcing that he would summon every citizen in town and swear them in as his posse to assist in removing Len Redfield from the jail and taking him to Tucson.

Upon hearing this, Undersheriff Scanland summoned every able-bodied man under the rule of *posse comitatus* to guard the jail against any unauthorized actions by Evans. When the citizens arrived, guards were stationed around the courthouse and jail on the outside to repel any attack that might be made by Evans's party. The main body of the citizens' force, numbering nearly one hundred men, filed into the jail yard. They took Scanland and jailer McKane prisoner and placed them under guard. Scanland and McKane were searched for the jail keys, and the key to the outside door was found in McKane's pocket. A search of the sheriff's office turned up the key to the inside lock.

Once the citizens were in the cell area, they threw ropes over two braces between a joist and then opened the cells. Joe Tuttle and Len Redfield were quietly taken out into the corridor. Redfield was game, so when the men went into the cell to bring him out he coolly looked around and asked, "Who is the leader of this gang?" As the noose was placed around his neck he remarked, "Well, boys, I guess my time has come."

Tuttle broke down completely when the men entered his cell. He placed his hands over his face and sobbed, "Let me talk; give me time to talk," and one of the men replied, "You didn't give poor Collins time to talk, and we will serve you the same way."

The noose was placed around Tuttle's neck. Both men were drawn up and the loose ends tied off. They did not struggle, even though they slowly strangled to death. After the two men were hanging, young Carpenter was brought out of his cell and told to look at his uncle and at Joe Tuttle and to take warning by their fate—he was young and could still turn from his course and make a man of himself. He was pale as a ghost when brought from his cell but recovered when assured that he would not be hanged. He was returned to his cell, and the mob guarded the hanging men until a physician pronounced them dead. They then disbanded and went about their business as though nothing happened.

An inquest soon followed, conducted by the local judge, the coroner being absent. The verdict? The two men had been hanged by persons unknown. The remains of Tuttle were buried in the town's cemetery just after sundown. Evans telegraphed Hank Redfield at Tucson informing him of the fate of his brother and asked for instructions on what disposition should be made of the body. The answer was to send it to Tucson, and on Monday evening Len Redfield's remains were sent in one of Eugene Cabott's wagons. On September 7 Wells, Fargo & Company paid Sheriff Doran the $600 reward for capturing Redfield and Tuttle.

<> <> <>

The pursuit of "Red" Jack Almer and Charles Hensley continued. They had traveled to a spring in the Rincon Mountains and then went on to a miner's cabin located 35 miles from Redfield's ranch. Sheriff Bob Paul went there, but the boys escaped in a hail of gunfire, leaving behind clothing, ammunition, supplies, and one horse. On Monday, September 24, Pete Mathews, a prospector in the Rincon Mountains, went down to Pantano and telegraphed Sheriff Paul that he had seen Almer and Hensley in camp on September 23 in a canyon about 1½ miles from Page's ranch. The lawmen struck the camp at first light on Tuesday and drove the men out of their blankets. Almer and Hensley managed to flee a second time, but again were forced to abandon all their provisions and equipment. They then headed for a Mexican ranch 18 miles above Redfield's, with Sheriff Paul and J. P. Gabriel close on their trail.

On Tuesday, October 2, news was received of the whereabouts of the fugitives, so George Martin, Wells, Fargo & Company's agent in Tucson, immediately notified Sheriff Paul and hired a locomotive to carry the posse to Willcox. The sheriff took with him deputy Alfredo Carrillo, T. D. Casanega, and George McClarty. On Tuesday morning Bob Paul went to the Percy brothers' ranch 10 miles northwest of Willcox and learned that the fugitives were expected there that night, even though it was storming very hard. The sheriff took Jim Percy, John McCluskey, and John Laird and set up an ambush by putting the men under the wagons of two trains camped nearby. At 9:00 P.M. Almer and Hensley approached the tailboard of one wagon and the sheriff called for them to halt. The fugitives started to run and commenced shooting. The whole posse fired a volley in the dark and the men fell, Almer within 20 feet of the wagon and Hensley 50 feet further away. About an hour after the shooting, McCluskey went to get his horse and heard Hensley riding off.

Almer had managed to crawl another 40 feet after he received a charge of buckshot in the pit of the stomach from McCluskey's gun. He also had a rifle ball through the right cheekbone just under the eye. The men could hear him groaning for five hours, but did not investigate in the dark as it could have been a ruse to expose the deputies to gunfire. The next morning they found Almer's body with his empty pistol by his head. His pockets were empty as well. Hensley had a .44 caliber model Winchester '73, but the cock had been shot off and it was partly broken in the night fight, so he took Almer's gun before abandoning his wounded partner. He had crawled on his hands and knees 400 yards to where he left his horse.

At daylight the posse started on Hensley's trail and followed it 8 miles. Hensley followed the telegraph poles toward Willcox 3 miles and then turned off into the mountains. He struck into a canyon and went over a ridge, and down on the other side into another canyon and followed it down about three-quarters of a mile. Paul told the boys to trail while he kept a lookout. The sheriff was ahead on the right hand side of the canyon as they went down when he saw Hensley's horse, saddled and bridled, standing between him and a pile of rocks. He called to the boys to circle around on the other side of the canyon. Casanega and McCluskey stayed with Paul while Carrillo, McClarty, Otto Moore, and a vaquero from Hooker's ranch, named Jimmie, went on the left side. The first the sheriff knew of Hensley's whereabouts was when Hensley shot at him from about 60 yards away.

Hensley was hidden behind a scrub oak, so all that could be seen was the smoke of his gun. He was down on the side of the gulch on Paul's side of the canyon, lying on his belly and shooting right up the hill toward the sheriff. The boys on the other side could see him plainly, though, so the shooting became general. Hensley continued to shoot until a bullet went through his heart and the men on the other side ran right down to where he lay. Carrillo halloed up to the sheriff, "Don't shoot, he's deader'n Hades."

Paul replied, "Don't go near him, he might shoot you."

Carrillo then took Hensley's gun away and saw that it was shot right through the stock and covered in dried blood. Beside the shot through his breast, Hensley had a gunshot wound in the left groin with clotted blood, a wound received the night before. When Carrillo got to Hensley, the man was lying on his belly. When he was rolled over, he was described as "perfectly white, there being no blood left in him." Carrillo said it appeared that, had they not found him, Hensley would have died of his wounds in a short time. He estimated that the pair had fired more than thirty shots during the wagon train battle, and Hensley had emptied "Red" Jack's Winchester rifle in the canyon fight, or about sixteen more shots. When searched Hensley had 55 cents in his pockets. Judge Nichols sent out a wagon and brought the bodies to Willcox for an inquest. The judge reported that the two fugitives had been "riddled with bullets."

Frank Carpenter, the last living member of the gang, apparently took the advice of the vigilantes too seriously. On November 22, 1883, the *Gazette* reported on Carpenter's death:

Frank Carpenter, who was recently admitted to bail in Florence on the charge of being an accessory to the Riverside stage robbery, and has been living on his ranch some twenty miles from Benson, died on Tuesday last from nervousness and fear. The hanging of Redfield and Tuttle has so worked on him that he imagined every person he met was going to hang him, which so affected his mind that he died of fright.

With all the principals and accessories dead, all that remained was to collect the reward. Sheriff Paul went into Florence in August 1884 and laid before the Board of Supervisors his claim for $600 for the capture of "Red" Jack Almer and Charles Hensley. They paid him accordingly. All the participants had died without telling what happened to the treasure, so it was never recovered.

CHAPTER THIRTEEN

ROBBERY AT SPEARFISH

There seemed little reason to rob a stagecoach in South Dakota after the Deadwood boom ended, but on February 17, 1894, that is just what two men did when they stopped the mail coach just outside Spearfish. It took many months, but finally they were tracked down, tried, convicted, and spent their next few years serving out their prison sentences at Sioux Falls.

In 1833 Ezra Kind led a party of seven men into the Black Hills in search of mineral wealth, and they discovered gold. Indians attacked the invaders at Spearfish Creek as the men were leaving the region with their riches, and when it became clear that they would all perish in the attack, Kind etched into a sandstone that they had found "all of the gold we could carry [on] our ponies."

In early May 1876, several small parties—among the first to invade Indian lands after gold was discovered at Deadwood Gulch— were searching for land to settle. They found what they were seeking on the banks of Spearfish Creek near the site of the Kind party's annihilation. A town was platted and patented on May 30, 1876, a month before the defeat of General G. A. Custer at the Little Bighorn. They named the town after the creek, which, in turn, had been named by Indians at least seventy-five years earlier and became known when they shared that name with fur trappers during the early 1800s. The Indian name characterized the clear, tumbling stream, which was the ideal spot to spear fish.

The town of Spearfish was nicknamed the Queen City because three surrounding mountain peaks—Lookout Mountain, Spearfish Mountain, and Crow Peak—seemed to form a crown above the valley. Spearfish was located at the mouth of Spearfish Canyon in Spearfish Valley. The lower elevation was ideal for agriculture, and the many farms built there provided the hay, feed, and produce for those living in the higher elevations.

In 1877, following the resolution of Indian title to the land, a store and post office were opened in the town, a school was established in 1883, and by 1890 the town had grown to nearly 700 people. Spearfish, although along the route of the Black Hills and Cheyenne Stage and Express Company, seemed immune from road agents. Coaches laden with heavy bars of Deadwood's gold bullion passed by with hardly any notice as road agents had found the perfect location to "jump" the coaches 100 miles south, below Robbers' Roost in Wyoming. However, in 1893 a railroad was completed through the canyon and the opportunity to take in a stagecoach at Spearfish, or further south in Wyoming, seemed lost forever.

◇ ◇ ◇

On a bitter cold Saturday an hour before midnight, February 17, 1894, Ernest Flynn was driving the mail buckboard from Miles City to Spearfish for contractor Tony Gerrig. Just as he turned the corner at the fairgrounds, which required him to slow the team, he said he saw two men suddenly appear in the road ahead. One was tall and dark complected, while the second man was described as a short, thick-set white man. The taller of the men seized the bridles of the team and pointed a revolver at Flynn's head while assuring him that he would not be harmed. The second man, according to the driver, also pulled a revolver as he stepped forward and, without speaking a word, began searching through the wagon bed for the mail pouch. He took out the pouch and cut the leather strap, then spilled the contents onto the ground—rifling through the contents, removing the letters, and returning the rest of the papers to the pouch before throwing it into the wagon.

Next he went through Flynn's pockets, and the unarmed driver put up no resistance as the robber took everything of value. When Flynn asked that his tobacco be returned, adding, "But take anything else you want," the tobacco was returned to his pocket. The taller robber then released the bridles and told Flynn to continue on, and Flynn did not hesitate. He whipped along his team the last 2 miles into Spearfish where he woke the postmaster and lawmen and reported the robbery. Meanwhile the robbers collected the letter mail from the ground and took it several miles from the road before going through it for money.

It was too dark and too cold to begin an investigation that night, so the men waited for Sunday morning. However, overnight a light snow fell, and by daybreak all the tracks were covered; the only clue was Flynn's description. It was impossible to determine immediately how much the road agents had stolen, but it was thought they had taken a substantial sum from the mails, possibly several hundred dollars, as there was no place in Miles City to purchase money orders and the numerous remittances to Montgomery, Ward & Company in Chicago always contained currency. On Sunday Postal Inspector M. C. Fosnes of Des Moines, Iowa, went to Spearfish to investigate and went out with a posse consisting of deputy U.S. Marshal Andrew Bray of Lead City, ex-Deputy Marshal Chris Mathieson, Deputy Sheriff W. P. Lindley, and City Marshal B. F. Lazzell. The party started its investigation at the scene, and the four lawmen continued searching for a trail or a clue while Fosnes returned to Deadwood.

During the time they searched for the fugitives, Fosnes began to suspect that Flynn was involved in the robbery. As early as February 26, he wrote to Spearfish postmaster, W. H. Todd:

Reflection revives and strengthens the idea with me that Flynn himself may after all have been concerned in the robbery, somehow, notwithstanding his fair reputation and apparent simplicity. Possibly he was a passive accessory—allowed a bolder man to cut and rifle the pouch, then divided the plunder. It would be interesting to know what familiars or cronies he has along the road. The Baxters might have enticed him into the scheme, for instance. . . . I think it will be well to keep a strict watch of Flynn; of course without hinting any suspicion to him, and I would therefore show this to no one but Mr. Lindley. Flynn may make some off-hand significant remark, or you may draw something from him by casual discreet questions. If completely reassured that he is not suspected, he may commit some act of self-betrayal.

It took some time and the shipment of a "dummy package" of money, which was delivered unmolested, before Fosnes was satisfied that Flynn was not involved. Another trail turned cold.

It had been reported that several days prior to the robbery two men of similar description had come into Spearfish, but had not been seen since Thursday. By Tuesday Frank White, a tall light-skinned African American, and his companion Isadore Ynojos, a thick-set, dark-complected Mexican, were arrested and lodged in the Deadwood jail. Fortunately for the two men, Fosnes was in Deadwood when they were arrested. They were arraigned before the U.S. commissioner, and Flynn could not identify either man. Following a brief but thorough investigation, Fosnes concluded that the two prisoners were not involved in the robbery. After Fosnes had gained the concurrence of the U.S. commissioner, both prisoners were released and the investigation continued.

Fosnes discovered that postal note no. 253 had been issued at Alzada, Montana, on February 16 and was included in the mails when stolen. He wrote to the postal inspector in Helena that he did not think the robbers would destroy the note and might have "passed over into Wyoming, perhaps through Sundance, and the note may have been cashed somewhere in that section of that state—and again, at some office in the Black Hills section of South Dakota." He was certain that when the note was cashed it would provide him a clue. When the note did not turn up, Fosnes wrote to the postal auditor to search for the stolen postal note among his returns, but it was never found among those that had been cashed.

Fosnes also determined that a letter mailed from Riverdale, Wyoming, was included in the mails that day, and it was believed to have been stolen, but it had been delivered to Dr. James B. Massie in Houston, Texas. It was thought that the robbers might have, for some unknown reason, posted the letter at another office later, but after careful investigation it could never be determined how this one letter had continued on, unless it had been among the papers returned to the coach. Another trail turned cold.

On March 1, 1894, Deputy Sheriff W. P. Lindley reported to Fosnes that he had not made much headway in the case but had been following up on a report that two men had gone into Spearfish about the time of the robbery and pawned a watch for goods. These two men, with another man, had pitched their tent in Higgins Gulch about 3 miles southwest of the fairgrounds and had with them one gray and three bay horses and a wagon, which was pulled by only two of the horses.

On Sunday they abandoned their campsite and left behind wood and water, but took their other belongings and moved to a deserted cabin 1½ miles north of the gulch. The two men who had pawned the watch seemed to generally match the description of the two robbers, so Lindley was trying to determine their whereabouts. He learned that all three men had departed on Monday in the direction of Sundance, Wyoming, and they were soon identified as C. A. Parsons, C. Wilson, and Charles Barber.

Since there was no way to tell which of the men or how many had been involved in the robbery of the mails, many months were spent, and numerous letters sent out by Fosnes, in trying to track down all three men. Finally, on October 8, they were all jailed, and all three were indicted for robbing the mails, but it was later determined that none of these men was involved in the Spearfish mail-coach robbery. The postal inspector was once again at a dead end in his investigation, but he never abandoned his search for clues.

In mid-July 1895 Fosnes received a letter from Columbus Shannon, then in the Hickory County Jail at Hermitage, stating that he knew of the robbery of the Spearfish mail wagon and the parties responsible. In Hickory County there were more than 300 people related in various ways to the Pitts family, and most of them were respectable citizens, but Shannon had shared a cell with Tom Pitts and learned from his cellmate the details of the Spearfish robbery. He wrote enough of the details to Fosnes to convince the postal inspector that he knew something of value. Fosnes arrived in Hickory County on August 2 and interviewed Shannon, when he heard for the first time the names Ulysses S. Pitts and George R. Hayes, who had been known as Dunn in South Dakota. Fosnes once again opened his investigation into the mail robbery.

Fosnes discovered that Ulysses's wife, Sallie C. Pitts, had once run off with cousin Tom Pitts. She returned in the summer of 1892, however, and the couple reconciled. Ulysses, who was apparently somewhat dim-witted, and Sallie then moved to South Dakota to put some distance between Sallie and Tom. The Pitts couple leased a ranch on the road between Miles City and Spearfish, 12 miles from Spearfish. Tom followed and took up a residence not far from them. Ulysses and Sallie took in a boarder named George Dunn, and soon Sallie and Dunn became intimate. Ulysses, who was aware of the arrangement, was unable to stop or discourage the affair. Mrs. Pitts left her husband in Late February, shortly after the robbery of the mail coach, and returned to Hickory County, Missouri. Soon after her departure the two men picked up stakes and followed her, and Tom Pitts was not far behind.

Fosnes charged Deputy U.S. Marshal W. T. Brown of Springfield, Missouri, with the responsibility of finding and arresting Pitts and Hayes and locating Sallie and Tom Pitts. When Sallie Pitts was found at work in a hotel in Springfield, Missouri, Fosnes hurried there and on August 6 recorded the sworn, signed statement of Mrs. Pitts. The wording in the affidavit reflects his interpretation. Sallie Pitts reportedly said:

On the Saturday night, in February 1894, that said mail stage was robbed, my husband and Dunn left home about one hour after dark, saying they were going hunting. They were on horseback. I was asleep and do not know the hour when they returned that night. The next day they told me that they had been over to the Spearfish fairgrounds and there held up the mail carrier, Ernest Flynn, and robbed the mail. They said they had blackened their faces. Dunn had a revolver at that time, but my husband had none, and their story of the robbery was that Dunn had stopped the horses and covered Flynn with his revolver while my husband got the mail. They claimed to have found $60 or $65 dollars in the mail. Dunn had the money, but I never saw any of it. While I had heard them discuss the project of a mail robbery, I had no idea that that was their errand when they left home that Saturday evening, else I should have done my best to dissuade my husband from the undertaking. He was inveighed into it by George Dunn, alias Hayes.

Fosnes next found Tom Pitts in Pittsburgh and on August 8 took his sworn, signed statement. Pitts stated that Ulysses had told him on the Tuesday following the robbery all the details of the hold-up and had since discussed it with him on numerous occasions, which were the same as related by Sallie Pitts. Both Sallie and Tom agreed to go to South Dakota and testify on behalf of Ulysses.

Deputy Marshal Brown sent out inquiries on Hayes, and the fugitive was located at Bolivar in Polk County, where he was employed on a threshing crew. He was arrested on August 9. The lawman, who knew Ulysses, found him at his father's home on August 12 and jailed him with Dunn in Springfield, but neither prisoner would make a statement except that Dunn admitted his true name was Hayes. Brown then suggested that Fosnes should charge the men under different sections of the U.S. Code, with Hayes under the more serious charge so that Pitts would be encouraged to confess and testify against his crime partner. The prisoners were taken up river on the *Milwaukee* under guard of the deputy marshal and John L. Gates, arriving at Sioux Falls on August 26. Sallie Pitts, with her four-year-old son, and Tom Pitts also went to Sioux Falls, where they took separate rooms at the Phillips House to maintain an appearance of propriety while they awaited the trial.

No time was wasted in returning an indictment against the two defendants, and a trial date was set within a week. The following day, Ulysses pled guilty to a charge of robbery of the mails, the lesser of two possible charges, which carried a penalty of five to ten years. Hayes, believing that he would also be charged with simple robbery, provided a full confession. He first said that he had stayed in the house the entire night of the robbery and that Ulysses and Sallie were responsible for the robbery. He claimed that Sallie had planned the robbery and at one time had become so frustrated with their delays in carrying it out that she donned men's trousers and went out to stop the coach, but returned empty handed. Hayes said, "Mrs. Pitts, her husband and the other Pitts are in a conspiracy to saddle the robbery off on me. . . . I did not seduce Mrs. Pitts but she seemed to have an attraction for me and when I went away, and discarded her, she got up this scheme for my punishment."

Hayes finally admitted his involvement and said that he and Ulysses had ridden 10 miles from their house to the place of the robbery, tied their horses out of sight from the road, and disguised their appearance by applying shoe-blacking to their faces. He insisted that his revolver was not loaded when he grabbed the reins, so that the life of the carrier was never in jeopardy. He then claimed that Sallie Pitts induced him to commit the robbery and took all the money and said he was going to plead guilty. However, when he learned that he had been indicted on the more serious charge of "robbing the mail by putting the life of the carrier in jeopardy by using a dangerous weapon," which carried a life sentence, he talked it over with his appointed lawyer, J. H. Snyder, and decided to plead not guilty. Negotiations over the next two days, however, resulted in an agreement to accept a plea of guilty to the lesser crime of simple robbery for Hayes as well, and this was submitted to the court on the August 29.

On August 30 Hayes was brought into court to be sentenced. When he stood, Judge Alonzo J. Edgerton observed that he had been indicted under a charge that carried a life sentence. He said that under those circumstances ten years was long enough and sentenced him to the maximum under the lesser charge agreed to by the district attorney. The following day Ulysses Pitts was brought into court and the judge sentenced him to the minimum term of five years, but it was understood that the district attorney would sign a petition to the president in one year asking for a pardon. The petition for Pitts was submitted and the pardon granted by President McKinley on July 7, 1897, after Pitts had served nearly two years. Hayes was not as fortunate as his petition for pardon was denied in 1898, and he was released after serving his entire sentence, less good time, on August 30, 1902.

Hayes claim of Mrs. Pitts's involvement was dismissed as a weak attempt to divert blame, and no charges were ever filed against her.

CHAPTER FOURTEEN

ARIZONA'S PETTICOAT BANDIT

There were many reports of women stagecoach robbers, including "Dutch" Kate and Lizzie Keith in California and the Harvey girls in Idaho. However, no female stagecoach robber could be substantiated until Pearl Hart stepped out of the brush in Pinal County, Arizona, in 1899 and stepped into history as the first "petticoat bandit." After a brief prison term Pearl became interested in another stage, and appeared as the Arizona Bandit in a play by that name at the Orpheus Theater in Kansas City. Pearl lived into her eighties and died Pearl Hart Bywater in Arizona.

In 1924 a petite, middle-aged woman walked into the old Pima County courthouse in Tucson, Arizona, and asked if she could have a tour of the jail facility, explaining, "I once was jailed here for a stagecoach robbery." The jailer looked her over carefully. Just about everyone was familiar with the story of Pearl Hart and had seen at least one of the many photographs taken of her as a young girl at the turn of the century. This was Pearl, all right, and she was given a tour of the entire jail, including the room from which she had escaped. She left, satisfied with her reminiscenses, and did not return.

<> <> <>

Pearl Taylor was born at Lindsay, Ontario, Canada, in 1871. During her finishing school years she was plain and plump, so when a dashing gambler showed her his undivided attention, she was easily infatuated. After several months nineteen-year-old Pearl and Brett Hart eloped.

Brett and Pearl moved about the Ontario countryside for several years, Brett plying his trade and both experiencing the financial ups and downs of the gambling profession. In 1893 the couple decided to attend the World's Columbian Exposition in Chicago where, Brett assured her, games of chance would make their fortune. Ignored by big-time gamblers, Brett finally settled on a job as barker in a sideshow. While Brett failed in his quest for financial security for his family, Pearl was more successful in her quest for entertainment, spending her days among the performers of the Wild West Show.

When the exposition ended, Pearl parted company with her husband, intent on seeing the West for herself. Pearl left Chicago for Trinidad, Colorado. It was rumored that her ticket had been bought by one of the show's cowhands who had taken a fancy to her figure. In Trinidad, Pearl gave birth to a boy, whose father was never identified. The *Arizona Star* later described her life at that time, "She wrestled with the world in a catch-as-catch-can style making a living for herself and her baby son."

Soon, however, she sent the boy to Canada to be raised by her mother and continued her travels westward, working her way from mining camp to mining camp taking whatever job presented itself. During these years she worked mostly as a cook or a housemaid. In 1895 Pearl and Brett met by chance in Phoenix, Arizona, and soon were together again. This time the relationship lasted several years and Pearl gave birth to a second child, a girl they named Pearl. However, during their separation Brett had developed violent tendencies. After a heated argument, he beat Pearl, then quickly absented himself to avoid arrest and joined the army. Pearl sent her young daughter to Canada for her mother to raise and resumed her camp following.

<> <> <>

In the spring of 1898 she took a job at the Mammoth Mining Camp. There she met Joe Boot, a miner, and a close friendship developed. When Joe announced that he was leaving for Globe to start a new job, Pearl agreed to go with him. In late summer of 1898, Pearl received a letter from her brother asking for money for her ailing mother. Pearl, who adored her mother, sent all her savings. When a second request came, Joe chipped in and sent his spare change as well. Pearl suspected she would soon need more money, so Joe suggested that they start a hauling company to take supplies to the Mammoth Mine. When this venture failed, they tried their hand at mining, and even struck a vein though it played out quickly.

Finally, the dreaded third request came, and Pearl was frantic. She needed money to send to her mother, but had none. It was then that Joe suggested they rob a stagecoach. Pearl reported later that she was at first reluctant, but Joe was persuasive. After all, he assured her, it was just this once to get enough money for her mother and then they would settle down in another territory to live a law-abiding life together. Pearl was finally convinced and they made their plans over a campfire that evening. There was no reason to delay, so before daybreak they set out. Pearl cut her hair to resemble a man's and tucked the ends under her sombrero. She donned a man's gray flannel shirt, Levis, and boots as her disguise. In her belt was tucked a well-oiled .38 caliber revolver. Joe sported a forty-five-caliber six-shooter and a sawed-off shotgun. They chose a point where there was a sharp bend in the road, which would require the driver to slow down, and there they took up positions in the brush.

On May 29, 1899, at 2 P.M., they heard the stage approaching and at that precise moment stepped out "with revolvers cocked and aim steady."

Joe called out, "Stop and elevate!"

Pearl, not to be left out, ordered, "Raise 'em!"

Joe covered the driver and told Pearl to search the passengers. She ordered the three passengers out and systematically took their valuables:

Pearl Hart
ARIZONA HISTORICAL SOCIETY, TUCSON, AHS #9183

She took $390 from a short, fat drummer named O. J. Neal; a tenderfoot contributed $36; and a Chinese man gave up $5. Pearl then pranced back and forth, trying to seem desperate, but finally gave each man a dollar "for grub and lodging," she said. She then ordered the passengers back into the stage and sent them on their way. Pearl and Joe were so new at the game that they had not thought to ask for the mail sacks or for the treasure box, an oversight that would later prove to Pearl's benefit.

Perhaps the robbers thought that they would not be recognized and the law would not know whom to pursue, but that was not the case. As soon as the stage driver pulled into Florence, Sheriff William C. Truman was told the details. The driver identified the culprits as Joe Boot and Pearl Hart, "who the driver recognized despite the fact that she looked like a young man." A posse was formed and the pursuit began.

<> <> <>

Pearl and Joe had not made plans for their escape beyond a determination to connect with the train at Benson. They realized that a posse would soon be on their trail so they zigzagged through unfamiliar country for two days, getting lost several times only to happen onto a familiar landmark. During that time they barely avoided the posse on a few occasions. Even the weather would not cooperate, and they were drenched in a downpour. The pair was only 20 miles from their destination when they bedded down beneath a stand of trees—exhausted, wet, and hungry. Sheriff Truman's posse found them there and quickly surrounded the sleeping pair of desperadoes. The lawmen moved in quietly and collected the robbers' firearms, which had been placed close at hand, before awakening them. Joe, seeing their situation, submitted. Pearl had other notions, however, and fought ferociously. Sheriff Truman later commented of Pearl after she was in jail,

One wouldn't think that she is a very tiger for nerve and for endurance. She looks feminine enough now, in the women's clothes I got for her, and one can see the touch of a tasteful woman's hand in the way she has brightened up her cell. Yet, only a couple of days ago, I had a struggle with her for my life. She would have killed me in my tracks could she had got to her pistol.

Pearl and Joe were lodged in the Florence jail, but Pearl was soon transferred to the jail at Tucson, a wing of the county courthouse. Pearl managed to break jail at 3:00 A.M. on October 12. The *Tucson Star* reported that the woman stage robber was a prisoner of Pinal County officials, but was taken from the Florence jail and brought to Tucson because the accommodations at the Pinal County jail were not suitable for women prisoners. Since her confinement Sheriff Wakefield and his deputies had used every precaution for her safekeeping and placed her in a room directly over the rear room of the county recorder's office. This room adjoined the small room containing the stairway leading up to the tower of the building with a door at the head of the stairs leading down to the main entrance. Between the two rooms there was nothing but a lath-and-plaster partition. The door leading into the tower from the courthouse was generally locked, but on the night of the escape it was left unlocked.

It was later surmised that, after everything was quiet, confederate Ed Hogan entered the courthouse, walked up the stairway, and entered the tower room through that unlocked door. It was then the work of but a very few minutes to cut a hole through the wall into Hart's room, where she was holding a sheet to catch the plaster that fell on her side. After the hole was cut, she put a table underneath and, placing a chair upon that, crawled through the hole. From the size of the aperture, it was evident that Pearl must have required considerable help in getting through. After she joined her accomplice in the escape, it was only necessary to open the door and descend the stairway into the street. Since there was no night watchman for the courthouse outside the jail, it was an easy matter to gain the street without detection. Hogan had tied horses nearby, and the pair made a beeline out of town.

When the jail was locked up on Wednesday night, Hogan was missing, and it was learned that he had hid himself in the city until about midnight and then returned to the county building to assist in the escape. Serving a sentence for drunk and disorderly conduct, he had but ten more days to serve and had been given some liberty as a trusty. It was probably Hogan who left the stairway door unlocked.

Sheriff Wakefield pursued the escaped bandit as far as Bowie and then returned to Tucson. Even though the pursuit in the Arizona Territory was discontinued, Pearl was free only a short time. She and Hogan were soon captured by legendary lawman George A. Scarborough of Deming, New Mexico, at an "outlaw hangout." Pearl was reportedly starting a gang "of which she was to be the bandit queen," and Hogan was her first subject.

In early November Pearl and Joe were tried for the stagecoach robbery. Joe pled guilty and was sentenced to thirty years at the Yuma Territorial Prison. He arrived there on November 11, 1899, and was registered as prisoner no. 1558. His record reveals that he was born in Ohio. Upon his arrival he was described as twenty-eight years of age, 5 feet 4 inches tall, 145 pounds, with brown eyes and black hair. His previous jobs included sailor and cook. He could read and write and did not drink or use drugs except tobacco. Joe worked hard at the prison and gained the confidence of the prison staff. He was given the job of driving food to the outside work crews, and on February 6, 1901, he drove his loaded cart through the front gate and continued on to freedom. Joe Boot was never heard of again.

Pearl was acquitted on the territorial charge of stage robbery. The *Arizona Sentinel* reported on November 25, 1899, that the "recent action of a jury at Florence, Ariz., in promptly acquitting, by a vote of 11 to 1, a female stage robber who had acknowledged her guilt in writing is not likely to do the woman much good, as she was immediately arrested on another charge." The new charge was for theft of the driver's pistol, as she had only been charged previously with theft of the passengers' money. The *Los Angeles Times* said of her defense, "In these days of women's rights the question of sex should not be allowed to play any greater part in crime than it is supposed to do in merit and achievement."

Upon acquittal on the charge of stagecoach robbery, the judge "roasted" the jury before he dismissed them. He then ordered that Pearl be rearrested on the charge of robbing the stage driver of his pistol. A jury was immediately impaneled, and she was tried, convicted of that crime, and sentenced to five years at the Yuma Territorial Prison.

Pearl arrived at the prison on November 17, 1899, and registered as prisoner no. 1559. She was described as aged twenty-eight years, 5 feet 3 inches in height, one hundred pounds, with gray eyes and black hair. She was reportedly literate, drank alcoholic beverages, and smoked tobacco. She also admitted to the use of morphine and claimed no legitimate occupation.

Pearl occupied the specially constructed women's quarters in the southwest corner of the prison, a cavelike dwelling carved into the cliff. The *Arizona Graphic* described her situation:

Pearl occupies a cell as large as an ordinary bedroom, which is excavated in the hill side, and she has a "houseyard" in which to take her constitutional whenever she is minded. She is evidently living on the fat of the prison, as there was a pound of butter on the table in her cell the morning I called on her. Several weeks of prison life had relieved physical system of its load of opium, for Pearl was a "hop fiend" of insatiable appetite, but her wicked face is sallow, for she has not been deprived of her cigarettes.

The prison secretary reported that during her incarceration "her record was excellent, and she devoted her entire time while in durance to making lace and fancy work which had a good sale among visitors here." He did not mention that she also wrote poetry, some of which was published.

Pearl aspired to perform on the stage and the *Yuma Sun* announced, in mid-1902 that:

Mr. and Mrs. C. P. Frizzle of Silver City, New Mexico, arrived in Yuma last Wednesday on a visit to Mrs. Frizzle's sister, Pearl Hart, the notorious female stage robber, who is serving a five year sentence in the territorial prison. Mrs. Frizzle is an actress and also a playwright, and has written a play entitled 'Arizona Bandit' in which Pearl Hart is to play a leading role.

The play will be put on the stage as soon as Pearl is released from prison, which will be early in 1904.

On December 15, 1902, the *Arizona Citizen* announced the parole of Pearl Hart. She was pardoned by Governor Alexander Brodie on the recommendation of the Board of Control and the prison's superintendent. Tucson's *Citizen* commented that the sudden release came as a surprise to every one familiar with the case and said, "In fact, it must have been an agreeable surprise to the prisoner, because she confidently expected to have to serve her full sentence." The pardon was granted on condition that Pearl remain outside the territorial boundary until the expiration of her sentence. Mr. and Mrs. Frizzle had moved to Kansas City, and Pearl's mother, with her two children, had joined them there to await Pearl's release. Yuma's *Arizona Sentinel* reported:

PEARL HART FREE

The Notorious Woman Bandit will Tackle the Stage Again, This Time as an "Actress" and Not As a Highway Robber.

Pearl Hart, the notorious, once more breathes free air, having been paroled by Governor Brodie last Saturday, and she left on Monday night's train for Kansas City. Quite a large number of people were at the depot to get a glimpse of Arizona's famous female ex-bandit and they were not disappointed for she was there, and if there is one thing more than another that Pearl is not "shy on" it is a fondness for notoriety.

Her ticket was bought straight through to Kansas City, where her mother and sister live, and the latter has written a drama in which Pearl will assume the leading role, arrangements having been made to play the Orpheum circuit, the initial performance to be given in Kansas City. It is understood that the drama will embody Pearl's own experience as a stage robber, with all the blood and thunder accompaniments, and the famous Pearl will once again, with her trusty Winchester, hold up the driver of a western stage, line up the passengers and relieve them of their valuables while her partner, "Boots," covers the victims with his gun and takes no

158

chances. . . . She leaves the prison in good health, and free from the opium habit, to which she was an abject slave on entering the prison. Pearl is a little woman weighing 105 pounds, but she has the slangy, tough demeanor, and when one contemplates her part in the stage robbery, it must be admitted that she has the nerve.

A later disclosure suggested that Pearl had become pregnant while in custody, and the suddenness of her pardon was the result. There is no record of a third child being born to Pearl, so the claim may have been a ruse to gain her early release—a rumor spread to justify her release or merely a misunderstanding on the part of a prison official.

After a brief career on the stage, Pearl managed a cigar store in Kansas City but, it seems, got into a bit of legal trouble again and moved to New York City. It was rumored that she worked in Buffalo Bill's Wild West Show for a time shortly before the start of World War I, though there was no record of her on the payroll. After the war she returned to Arizona where she met and married a rancher named Calvin Bywater, and they settled near Globe, Pinal County. Pearl Hart Bywater died on December 30, 1955, at the age of eighty-five.

CHAPTER FIFTEEN

GOLD AT THE END OF THE RAINBOW

While Pearl Hart was the first woman to serve time in prison for stagecoach robbery, she was not the last. Mollie Burget was involved in the robbery of the Durkee, Oregon, stagecoach on April 5, 1915. Burget, Joe Carlson, and "Sourdough" Bill Halter were sentenced to serve terms in the state prison at Salem.

Beginning in 1843 thousands of emigrants traveled west on the Oregon Trail intent on settling the Oregon Country, then under shared ownership with Britain. In 1861 Henry Griffin, a member of a Mormon party, explored the area off the trail and discovered gold 8 miles west of present-day Baker City, 40 miles northwest of the Rainbow Mine established in 1901. The Griffin party mined the placers in the area they named the Mormon Basin, but there was not enough water in Dixie and Basin Creeks, especially during the hot summer months, so the work was entirely seasonal. Still, with the promise of a fortune in gold waiting to be picked up from the ground, boomtowns literally sprang from the earth. By 1862 Auburn boasted a population of more than 5,000. With mining so difficult, however, many local settlers turned to farming and established stores, with their primary customers the large transient miner population.

In 1862 the Express Ranch, a Wells, Fargo & Company stagecoach station, was established on the Durkee family ranch along the Umatilla to Boise Basin Stage and Freight Road. On April 21, 1865, the Express Ranch was designated a post office, with C. W. Durkee appointed the first postmaster, but the post office was soon moved to Weatherby. In 1883 the advancing railroad, following the natural path of the Oregon Trail, bought the right-of-way across the Durkee family farm and renamed the Express Ranch station Durkee. The railroad built a depot at Durkee, so, with a stagecoach station and railhead there, a town soon grew up around the site. On February 26, 1902, another post office was established there.

The placers were soon exhausted by panning, rockers, and sluices, so hydraulic equipment was brought in to excavate the hills. When this method failed to produce a profit, dredges, rockers, and screens followed. Once all the surface placers were extracted, which took several decades, the men turned their attention to the source of those placers—the veins of gold-bearing quartz buried beneath the hills—which required that shafts be dug. Discovery of the cyanide process in 1889 made the mining of gold-bearing quartz profitable. When a substantial vein of gold quartz was discovered above Rainbow Gulch in 1901, not far from Durkee, the digging quickly progressed to a depth of 200 feet. The mine had been idle and the old shaft flooded when, in 1911, it was leased by The United States Smelting, Refining & Mining Company of Boston. During the early months of that year, they sent their Colorado man, Howard Lee, to operate, explore, and develop the mine.

Superintendent Lee's wife, Mabel, joined him in July. Mrs. Lee arrived at the rail depot in Huntington, and the couple drove their wagon 18 miles to Rye Valley, a tiny village that served as the metropolis for Mormon Basin. Running over flat, dry land with only sagebrush on the landscape, the trip was interrupted occasionally by a curious gopher, a jackrabbit, or a rattlesnake. Once the couple reached the Mormon Basin, they were surrounded by green fields of oats and rye, and meadowlarks, singing in the poplars and cottonwoods.

The town of Rye Valley was the depot for the Huntington Stage Line, and the horses were changed there for the long ascent of Rye Valley Hill. After dinner the couple headed their wagon toward the Rainbow Mine, which was a steady climb of 10 miles over rough roads to the 5,000-foot level. There were only fifteen men working at the camp and living in a few rough cabins at that time, but the old mill building and superintendent's house were still in good repair. Lee's plan, if his exploration justified it, was to dig a new shaft and build a fifteen-stamp mill and cyanide plant to treat a hundred tons of ore daily. To accomplish this he would have to bring in water from the old shaft until he could cap the spring above the camp and also bring in electricity from Huntington, contract for timber and cord wood from the San Pedro Mountain wood lot, and build more living quarters for the men and their families before he could begin to assemble his crew of 250 to 300 miners.

Lee's exploration justified the investment, even though the Rainbow had no well defined lodes but instead followed an irregular vein system called breccia. By 1913 the force of miners at the Rainbow had grown to over 300 men, and the shaft, at 200 feet, had produced $250,000. Work had begun on sinking the shaft to 300 feet, and there were already plans to dig to 400 feet in the hope of finding a main ore body.

<> <> <>

At the foot of the last steep rise to the mine, 4 miles distant and just off company land, Mollie "Ol' Mol" Burget, usually misspelled Burgett, ran a notorious honky-tonk in Rainbow Gulch, frequented by most of the men from the mine. Lee tried in every way to close down Burget's place, but to no avail. He posted notices that drinking on the job would not be tolerated and stated that any man who reported for his shift while under the influence of liquor would be fired immediately. The men, in response to the threat of termination, simply stayed at Burget's place when they were drunk, so that crews often ran short. Holidays were the worst of it, and he tried offering bonus pay to those who showed up sober.

He refurbished the old mill building into a recreation hall and named it the Rainbow House, but miners were a suspicious lot so this strategy failed completely until he turned over the selection of entertainment to a committee of workmen. Even then the recreation hall was successful on those rare occasions when entertainment could be coaxed in.

When the ongoing conflict between Burget and Lee began seriously lowering morale at the mine, Lee tried religion and brought in clergy from Baker to preach to the men, but this also had no effect. Baker County Sheriff R. Price Anderson listened sympathetically to Lee's complaints, but felt he could do nothing legally to help with the situation.

<> <> <>

On Monday morning, April 5, 1915, Lee shipped $7,000 in gold bullion from the week's "clean-up" to the American Express office at Durkee, to be forwarded by rail to the assay office at Selby, California. Since the Rainbow had recently received a great deal of publicity as Oregon's most productive mine, Lee was afraid the stagecoach might be robbed, so he had taken the precaution of packaging his shipments in different ways. Some days he went so far as to send nothing but rocks or waste in the express box.

Ralph "Slim" Moorehouse was driving the Rainbow-to-Durkee stage that morning and received the load of gold in the shape of a seventy-five-pound cone, which was wrapped in a gunny sack to further disguise its appearance. However, there was no disguising the fact that it took two men to load the shipment on the coach, and this was a sure sign it was a heavy load of gold. Mrs. A. H. Freitag of Durkee, the only passenger, boarded just before 9:00 A.M., and the coach was off on time. In less than a half hour, the coach was just rounding a sharp curve in the road halfway between the mine and Rye Valley, which required the team to slow, when it was stopped by a diminutive man wearing a blue bandana mask and black serge coat.

The road agent suddenly appeared in the middle of the road, pointed his revolver at the driver, and announced, "Hands up! Hand over that gold, Slim."

The driver did not hesitate, took the gunny sack from beneath his legs, and threw it out. Moorehouse was then told to drive on and not look back. The passenger was not molested, or even acknowledged.

Moorehouse had not driven 200 yards when he defied the order and looked back to see a medium-sized man, wearing a white handkerchief for a mask, hidden behind a tree pointing a pistol at him. Mrs. Freitag continued to watch as the driver whipped up the horses and hurried into Rye Valley. She saw the men, on foot, carry the gold toward Pedro Mountain.

In town Moorehouse telephoned the mine with a report of the robbery. He told Lee that the robber who had confronted him wore light-colored trousers, a light hat, a black serge coat and vest. He noted that the robber knew him, referring to him by his nickname. Moorehouse then turned the stagecoach run over to another driver and remained at Rye Valley to join the posse that he knew would be organized quickly. He also telephoned Sheriff Anderson to report the robbery and told the lawman that he had a clue to the identity of one of the robbers, whom he identified as having a voice exactly like Joe Carlson's.

Carlson was a thirty-year-old man who was a petite 5 feet tall. His size matched that of the robber in the road. Carlson was known to be close friends with Molly Burget and a man named Halter, usually misspelled Halder.

Sheriff Anderson, upon hearing of the robbery, telephoned the marshal at Huntington and told him to arrest any suspicious persons arriving by stage. William "Sourdough Bill" Halter had been walking on the road not far from the scene of the robbery only a short time afterward, when he waved down and boarded the coach bound for Huntington. The Huntington stagecoach was about twenty minutes behind the Durkee coach and traveled on the same road for that part of its route. When Halter got to Huntington and the circumstances of his boarding the coach were related to the officer, he was arrested. The prisoner at first protested his innocence, perhaps a bit too loudly, but soon he confessed to his part in the robbery. He named Carlson as the small robber in the road and blamed him for the robbery, but also implicated Molly Burget as an accessory to the crime.

Sheriff Anderson, with Deputy Robert Nelson, commandeered Charles Olds's automobile and, after arming the posse, started for the scene of the robbery. They stopped in Rye Valley to pick up Moorehouse and headed toward Pedro Mountain, with the others of his posse following closely behind. Lee notified his superiors, and the insurance company posted a $1,000 reward for capture and conviction of the robbers. Lee and A. H. Hamilton, master mechanic at the mine, hurriedly armed themselves and started for the scene from the opposite direction. Sheriff Ben Brown of Malheur County, when he heard of the robbery, assembled a force of men. Soon there were three posses combing the hills between the site of the robbery and Pedro Mountain.

Sheriff Anderson saw from the tracks that the robbers remained afoot after they were out of Mrs. Freitag's sight, and he believed that they would have buried the gold and come back for it later, so he put a large part of his force to work scouring the hills for the plunder. On the evening of April 7, posse men found foot tracks and followed them to a giant sagebrush not more than 1 mile from the scene of the robbery. Beneath the growth they found the gold cone buried in a large badger hole—poorly disguised beneath dirt, rocks, and brush. Nearby they found the robber's small-sized black coat, blue mask, hat, gun, and cartridges. The posse prepared a fake brick resembling the shape of the gold bullion, replaced it in the gunnysack, buried it, and hid a man nearby to watch.

The posses had not yet learned of Halter's confession implicating Burget, but Lee suggested that "Ol' Mol" might have something to do with the robbery, or at least he hoped she had. As a result, Sheriff Anderson sent Deputy Nelson to investigate. Burget, who was forty-eight years old but looked much older, lived with thirty-year-old Joe Carlson in a dilapidated cabin in Miller. Deputy Nelson went to the cabin to search for clues. When the deputy asked to see Molly's gun, she acted surprised to find it missing from under her mattress. Later Burget's revolver was identified as the gun found near the badger hole.

Anderson was already confident that he had probable cause to make an arrest, so, at 4:00 P.M. on April 7, he took Carlson and Burget into custody at Miller and lodged them in the Baker County Jail. Halter was formally charged in the Huntington jail and moved by train to the Baker jail to await the next session of the grand jury. Halter, as soon as he got into the Baker jail, confided that he had hidden his gun near the scene of the robbery and offered to go with the officers to recover it. Marshal Ed Hanson and ex-Sheriff Ed Rand took the prisoner to a place where they recovered the firearm, a .32 caliber automatic pistol, from beneath a rock not 100 yards from the road. By 10:00 P.M. Halter was back in his cell and the officers, who had hoped they might get some other clues from Halter, learned nothing more while traveling to and from the scene. The officers also tried to get some admission from Burget and Carlson, but they would not weaken. During the weeks that followed, the honky-tonk was taken apart, board by board, in a fruitless search for additional clues.

The three prisoners were indicted by the U.S. grand jury and scheduled for trial in the circuit court within days. Carlson was tried first and convicted on April 24 of robbery by "putting the driver in fear," but not of the more serious offense of being "armed with a dangerous weapon which put the life of the mail carrier jeopardy," which carried a life sentence. When told of Carlson's conviction, Molly told the Baker *Morning Democrat*, "Well, that means Bill and I are up against it, too."

The joint trial of Halter and Burget commenced on June 25, and the evidence showed clearly that the woman was the brains behind the criminal plot. Halter testified that Burget stood on a hilltop near her cabin to observe what was being loaded onto the stage and to determine when the stage left the mine so she could signal the two robbers to be prepared for its arrival. Burget, who for the first time since her arrest seemed nervous while on the witness stand, had the presence of mind to

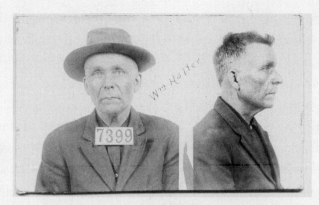

William Halter

Molly Burget

Joe Carlson

OREGON STATE ARCHIVES, DEPARTMENT OF CORRECTIONS, PHOTOGRAPHS 7398, 7399, 7400

implicate a man named W. G. "Ed" McCoy and tried to blame him and Superintendent Lee for the robbery. However, McCoy's alibi was well corroborated, and he could not be shaken on cross-examination.

The trial lasted two days. At 11:55 P.M., after three hours of deliberation, the jury returned verdicts of "guilty as charged" against the two defendants. The verdict would have come in earlier if two jurors had not held out for the more serious offense against Halter, that of using a dangerous weapon and putting the life of the mail carrier in jeopardy. Several days after the verdict was read, the three convicted robbers were brought into court for sentencing. The judge sentenced them to the state penitentiary "for a period of time without limitation, not less than three years nor more than fifteen years." On her sentence, Mollie said "I've lived a fast life. Now I'm forty-eight years old and unattractive, so I guess the pen is as good as any place."

<> <> <>

In June, only two months after the robbery and even before the trial commenced, the annual audit of the mine was conducted. The conclusion was that the company then operating the mine would let its lease expire in the fall and the property would revert to the owner, the Commercial Mining Company. The owner announced that a much smaller work force would be kept employed at the mine, but production had clearly peaked the previous year and it seemed unlikely that any new ore body or veins of gold-bearing quartz would be found. It was the end of the Rainbow.

On July 1, 1915, Carlson, Halter, and Burget were received at the Oregon State Prison in Salem. Carlson was registered as prisoner no. 7398, Halter as 7399, and Burget as 7400. Thirty-two-year-old Carlson, who had been born in Utah, was taller than first thought being nearly 5 feet 7 inches in height and weighing 135 pounds; he had blue eyes, sandy hair, and a "florid" complexion. Halter, who was born in Wisconsin, was fifty-seven years old, 5 feet 7½ inches tall and weighed 150 pounds; he had blue eyes and black hair turning gray. Burget, who had been born in Iowa, was forty-eight years old, 5 feet 3½ inches tall and weighed 163 pounds; she had gray eyes and dark brown hair.

The housing of women in prison during the early days of the twentieth century was troublesome. On July 21, 1916, after serving slightly more than one year, Burget was conditionally pardoned by the governor. On July 1, 1918, after serving the minimum sentences of three years, Carlson and Halter were paroled. Halter was not heard of again, but Burget, then using the name Kate Burget, and Joe Carlson reunited in San Francisco where they stayed out of trouble until 1928. In about April of that year, Burget's adult daughter was shot and killed, and Burget was believed to be a party to the killing. The mother collected several hundred dollars in insurance money, even though Carlson claimed that Burget did the shooting to save his life when the girl was shooting at him.

CHAPTER SIXTEEN

THE LAST STAGECOACH ROBBERY IN THE WEST

A few months after the sixtieth anniversary of the first stagecoach robbery, the last western stagecoach robbery occurred at Jarbidge, Nevada, and the driver was murdered in cold blood. Ben Kuhl was convicted of the murder and robbery, primarily on the basis of a bloody palm print—the first time a palm print was entered into evidence in a United States criminal prosecution. Kuhl was sentenced to death but was spared an ignominious end when his sentence was commuted to life in prison.

In 1916 Ben Kuhl was nearly broke and had accrued a substantial debt resulting from a failed attempt to jump a lot next to the post office earlier that year. Oscar and Ernest Hayes owned the lot upon which a small cabin was located. They moved the cabin off the lot and then had it graded in anticipation of building a much larger building, but the lumber had not arrived so the lot remained vacant. A sign was posted that a building would be constructed on that site as soon as the lumber arrived. One morning the Hayes brothers found a tent pitched on their lot. Ben Kuhl was living there and claimed ownership by occupancy. He was quickly evicted, charged with trespass, and fined $400. When he heard the judgment, he made some derogatory remarks about the "kangaroo court." This resulted in a fine of $50.

Kuhl was an easy man to dislike, and even the man with whom he shared a business interest referred to him as his partner, but never as his friend. Still, one of the town's tramp dogs attached himself to Kuhl and followed him everywhere. Kuhl, who did little to encourage the dog, also did nothing to discourage it. Perhaps the dog was his only friend.

<> <> <>

The mines around Jarbidge in Nevada were thriving at that time. Any time a stagecoach came into town there seemed a good chance that it would be carrying a substantial amount of treasure. The *Elko Independent* observed:

There is a steady and substantial increase in the payrolls of the camp; the Long Hike is pushing development work with the usual number. The O. K. is running along steadily, the Tacoma interests have let contracts on several claims, and Mr. Wingfield's engineers are doing considerable work. With these three big interests at work there is every assurance that next season will be a very active one for the Jarbidge District.

On December 5, Fred W. Searcy loaded his mail wagon at Rogerson, Idaho, and started for Jarbidge in a blinding snowstorm. Searcy was thirty-two years old but without a family of his own, though he had been previously married. He kept in touch with his mother, who lived in Washington, and his sister, who had recently moved to Independence, Missouri. For some time he had been driving the parcel-post wagon, so when in mid-November the postmaster promoted him to drive the mail wagon, he immediately wrote to his family to let them know of his advancement. Well thought of by everyone in town, Searcy was determined to deliver the mails on time and show that he was dependable in his new assignment.

Searcy bundled up tightly and hunkered down on the seat. He came upon several teamsters on the road near the summit, and it took some time and effort for them to maneuver past one another. When Searcy came along, they all moved aside and allowed him to pass on through so he could keep on schedule.

In Jarbidge Kuhl had made his plans carefully. He donned his overcoat and made sure he had a bone-handled .44 caliber revolver and penknife. He started out for the road and sneaked past Campbell's freighter camp and then went around Mrs. Dexter's house to a clump of brush on the side of the road. There, with the tramp dog camped nearby, he settled in to await the arrival of Searcy.

The coach arrived just before 6:30 P.M., in the midst of a blizzard. Kuhl came out of the brush after the wagon passed and climbed over the rear brake beam and onto the load. Without any warning he pulled his pistol, placed it behind Searcy's left ear, and pulled the trigger, but it only snapped. The wind covered the misfire, so he pulled the trigger again. This time the gun exploded in his hand, firing a single round. The bullet passed entirely through Searcy's head and came out his mouth, knocking out two lower teeth. Death was instantaneous, and Kuhl had to grab Searcy to keep him from falling out of the wagon. The team, startled by the sound of the shot, swerved to the right 4 feet and nearly went over the grade while Kuhl was struggling to pull Searcy's body into the wagon bed. Searcy's head dangled outside the wagon for some distance leaving a blood trail.

After the wagon traveled 75 feet, Kuhl was able to climb onto the seat, grab the reins, and steer the team back into the middle of the road. Kuhl hunkered down against the wind, wrapping himself tightly in his overcoat as he drove the wagon past Mrs. Dexter's house. She saw the mail wagon and called out to Searcy, but Kuhl did not respond. She assumed he couldn't hear her, even though he was only 15 feet away. Next he passed Campbell's camp where the freighter also called, "Hello, Kid," to Searcy, but again Kuhl pretended not to hear him. Campbell dismissed this action, thinking the man, too frozen and too long seated behind the team to respond, or perhaps he was asleep and let the team find its way to the barn.

Kuhl drove to where the old road, which used to cross the river before the bridge was built, forked off and followed it for 200 yards to a large stand of brush where he stopped the team. The dog had followed the wagon, trying to stay close to Kuhl. Kuhl pulled Searcy's body from the wagon bed and replaced it on the seat, positioning it so that it appeared as if he had slumped over while driving. He went through the second-class mailbag but found nothing of value. He then took the first-class mailbag and registered mail pouch and went to a dense thicket of brush where he could use a light, and examined every piece of mail carefully before discarding it. He found two packages for the Crumley & Walker's Success Bar and Café containing $3,000 and $200 respectively. There was also a package of $200 in change for the café and a package for H. Braunning containing $1,000 in cashier's checks, which were worthless to the robber. In all he got about $4,000 for his trouble, but there was no payroll.

He then went to the river and washed blood from his hands, removed his shirt, which he thought might have a bloodstain, and, tying a rock inside, sunk it in the river. He then took off his overcoat, which he believed might also have blood on it, threw it under the bridge, and buried a sack of silver nearby. Kuhl, now without a coat, hurriedly returned to his cabin, the dog still following him closely.

<> <> <>

When Searcy did not arrive at the expected time, the postmaster, Scott Flemming, hired Frank Leonard to take a packhorse and go out on the road to meet the coach, determine the trouble, and, if necessary, bring in the registered and first-class mail. He went out and searched but could find no sign of the wagon, team, or driver. At 9:00 P.M. the teamster, Campbell, went to the post office and reported his sighting of Searcy at 6:30 P.M., so the men went to the barn expecting to find him there with the wagon. When nothing was found, the townspeople formed parties and began to search the surrounding area. Men who went across the bridge found nothing, so they returned and spread out to find some clue.

The team was first seen and then the wagon. Searcy was on the seat, on the right by the brake as he would be if he was driving, but leaning to the left and only partially on the seat. He was frozen stiff, having been there about five hours. The men unhitched the team, sent the animals to the barn, and then carefully worked the wagon out of the brush. They did not believe that the team would have strayed to that location if Searcy had frozen to death on the seat, not with the barn so close, so they examined the wagon carefully.

They first noticed that the mailbag was missing and, suspecting foul play, examined the body again, more closely, this time noticing the frozen blood clots on his head and clothes. They searched the surrounding area and found the two second-class mailbags cut open with the contents rifled, and large and small footprints as well as a dog's track. It was too late and too dark to search further, so care was taken not to obliterate any sign as they extricated themselves from the scene.

Early the next morning, there were many men on the trail. A hunter carefully blew the fresh snow from the dog tracks and, upon careful examination, was certain that they were of a tramp dog that was always about the town. There were only a few large dogs in the camp, and the track was clearly the track of this dog. They found the dog and took him near the footbridge at 10:00 A.M. when, as expected, he followed the same trail. On the way the dog stopped where the first-class mail sacks were hidden in a dense thicket of brush, completely covered with snow. Here the men collected the discarded letters, finding on one of the pouches a bloody palm print, which they carefully preserved. They next tried to figure out to whom the dog might have been following, and several men knew that it had recently attached itself to Ben Kuhl.

Kuhl was arrested at 1:00 P.M. During a short hearing he denied the charge and brought witnesses who were supposed to clear him, but his alibi failed, and he was jailed. Meanwhile the search party had found the overcoat cached under the bridge. They looked about the area and found the sack of silver, which had contained $200—$18 had been removed. With it was a package of registered letters. The coat was

Ben Kuhl

quickly brought to the hearing and Kuhl denied it was his, but later his partner, who was working at the Long Hike Mine, came in and identified it as Kuhl's coat. The jackknife in the pocket looked like one belonging to Kuhl but could not be positively identified. Kuhl's cabin was searched and his gun was found, with one cartridge snapped and one expended, but the prisoner denied the gun was his. This gun, it turned out, had been in the possession of a man named William McGraw, a large man, who was partners with a smaller man named Ed Beck. These men were then arrested. Later a shirt was found sunk in the river. The water had washed out any bloodstains, but the laundry marks looked similar to those of Ben Kuhl.

Searcy's body was prepared and shipped to his sister in Missouri. On December 12 preparations were being made to take Kuhl, McGraw, and Beck to Elko to be lodged in the county jail. Sheriff J. C. Harris and District Attorney Edward P. Carville arrived at Elko on train No. 5 on December 14 while federal postal agents were sent to Jarbidge to continue the investigation. When the case was called in, Judge Errol J. L. Tabor's district court on September 18, 1917, each of the men had been granted a separate trial. At the judge's request the newspapers agreed to refrain from publishing any of the testimony until the third trial, so as not to prejudice jurors in the second and third trials. E. E. Caine was appointed to defend Kuhl, as he had no funds.

Kuhl's case was called first. The court began taking testimony on December 22, and by December 29 was embroiled in a battle over the palm print. The defense admitted the reliability of fingerprints but would not concede that a palm print was reliable for the purposes of identification. The judge, after arguments, noted that three cases had been decided and appealed since fingerprints were first admitted as evidence on February 11, 1911, in the Thomas Jennings murder case in Illinois, which was affirmed by the Illinois Supreme Court on December 21, 1911. He noted, however, that in Nevada no case had addressed the issue of fingerprints as evidence, and nationally no case had addressed palm prints as evidence. After carefully considering all the expert testimony and other factors, Judge Tabor allowed the palm print to be admitted to evidence, as well as enlargements of the print for display to the jury. The prosecution believed the print would positively identify Kuhl as one of the murderers, perhaps the principal murderer, as Beck and McGraw might only be accessories.

The admission of the palm print drew a great deal of attention, and it also extended the trial. Closing arguments did not proceed until the afternoon of October 5, the case having already consumed seventeen days of the court's time. On Saturday, October 6, the eighteenth day, the case went to the jury at 8:45 P.M. After two hours of deliberation, the jury found Kuhl guilty of murder in the first degree without recommendation, which meant he would have to suffer the death penalty and had only to choose between hanging and shooting as the means. He chose shooting and was taken to the prison to await the date in January 1918.

The trial of McGraw commenced on Monday, October 8, while E. E. Caine was already busy preparing an appeal in the Kuhl case. McGraw turned state's evidence, testified against Beck, and was released from custody. Beck was tried next, convicted as an accessory, and sentenced to life in prison.

A stay in the execution was granted in December 1917 when Kuhl's case was appealed to the state's Supreme Court contesting the validity of the palm print as a means of identification and challenging the expert status of those who testified to the comparison of the print and the copy of Kuhl's palm print. The Supreme Court heard the case on March 2, 1918, and on September 6 upheld the decision of the trial court. The court also ordered the lower court to have Kuhl appear and set a new date for his execution. Kuhl was again sentenced to die by firing party, this time on December 20, 1918. As the date for the execution neared, Kuhl, miscreant to the last, provided a self-serving, fabricated confession:

A few days before the robbery I had told Searcy that I needed money to develop several mining claims I had in the area of Jarbidge, but was unable to get it. Searcy then suggested that I could get the money by holding up the stagecoach. Searcy said he had done the same sort of thing in Idaho earlier and got away with it, so it would be easy to do again. The entire thing was a frame-up between Searcy and myself and we picked a point about a mile and a half from town. I had no gun so went to Beck, but he had none so I finally got one from McGraw. I climbed up on the wagon as agreed and we discussed the job, but Searcy said I could have the bag of silver worth $300 but not the $2,800 in greenbacks in the mailbag. Searcy tried to double-cross me, went for his gun, and in that last *moment I had to shoot in self-defense. I then proceeded to rob the mails of the $2,800.*

Kuhl said he could not remember if he slit open the mailbags or if they were already slit open.

The Board of Pardons had received thousands of letters asking that they commute Kuhl's death sentence to life imprisonment, and most of those who wrote did not know Kuhl, Searcy, or the facts of the case. Many were simply against the death penalty in any circumstance. Ed Beck, after having an opportunity to discuss the matter with Kuhl in prison, made statements that later corroborated Kuhl's last-minute confession. The board took into consideration the letters and must have given some credit to the prior statements of Beck and the confession because on December 13. One week before Kuhl was to die, it commuted his sentence to life imprisonment. The confession, an obvious self-serving fabrication, did serve a purpose, however, as it showed that the palm print evidence was reliable, a conclusion already reached by the Supreme Court. The print offered in evidence was in fact the print of Kuhl as claimed by the prosecution.

Beck was paroled in 1923 after serving only six years, but Kuhl remained in prison until May 1945 when, at the age of 61, he was released. The money he stole, except for the bag containing $178 in silver coins, was never found. Kuhl was not heard of again, though there were several romanticized tales of how he spent his final days.

BIBLIOGRAPHY

GENERAL REFERENCE

Elman, Robert. *Badmen of the West.* Secaucus, N.J.: Castle Books, 1974.

Nash, Jay R. *Encyclopedia of Western Lawmen & Outlaws.* New York: Da Capo Press, 1994.

Thrapp, Dan L. *Encyclopedia of Frontier Biography* (three volumes). Lincoln: University of Nebraska Press, 1988.

CHAPTER 1
THE FIRST STAGECOACH ROBBERY IN THE WEST

American Medical Association. Historical Register of Physicians.

Arnold, Oren. "The West's First Stage Robbery." *True Western Adventure* 1 (1957): 10.

Jackson, Joseph H. *Bad Company.* Lincoln: University of Nebraska Press, 1977.

Huffaker, Clair. "The First Stagecoach Robbery," SAGA, February 1956, 20–23.

Hume, James B. and John N. Thacker. *Report of Wells, Fargo & Co.'s Express, Nov. 5, 1870 to 1885.* San Francisco: H.S. Crocker & Co., 1885.

National Archives Records Administration. Old Military and Civilian
    Records: Veterans Roster for the Mexican-American War.
Secrest, William B. *Perilous Trails, Dangerous Men.* Clovis, Calif.: Quill
    Driver Books, 2001.

Newspapers:

Daily Evening Bulletin (San Francisco, Calif.): August 20, 1856; August
    22–23, 1856; August 26–28, 1856; September 13, 1856; September
    18, 1856; October 4, 1856; October 6, 1856; October 8, 1856;
    October 13, 1856.

CHAPTER 2
BALDY GREEN—THE JEHU

Block, Eugene B. *Great Stagecoach Robbers of the West.* Garden City,
    N.Y.: Doubleday & Company, 1962.

Newspapers:

Carson Daily Appeal (Nev.): May 23, 1865; May 26, 1865; May 30, 1865;
    June 13, 1865; August 15–17, 1865; September 8–9, 1865;
    September 13, 1865; September 22, 1865
Territorial Enterprise (Virginia City, Nev.): September 7, 1867; June 12,
    1868; July 4, 1868; July 6–7, 1868; November 17, 1872.

CHAPTER 3
THE ROBBERY AT PORTNEUF

Block, Eugene B. *Great Stagecoach Robbers of the West.* Garden City,
    N.Y.: Doubleday & Company, 1962.
Idaho State Historical Society Reference Series: nos. 147, 612, 679.
Langford, Nathaniel P. *Vigilante Days & Ways.* Missoula: Montana State
    University Press, 1957.

Leonard, Stephen J. *Lynching in Colorado, 1859–1919.* Boulder: University of Colorado Press, 2002.

Wilson, R. Michael. *Murder & Execution in the Wild West.* Las Vegas, Nev.: Rama Press, 2006.

Newspapers:

Idaho Statesman (Boise, Idaho): July 20, 1865; July 27, 1865; January 18, 1866; April 16, 1922.

Rocky Mountain News (Denver, Colo.): January 13, 1866.

Salt Lake Telegraph (Utah): August 24, 1864.

CHAPTER 4
STEPHAN VENARD

Secrest, William B. "When the Ghost Met Steve Venard," *Old West Magazine,* Fall 1968, 20.

"Steven Venard, Nevada County Pioneer." *Nevada Historical Society Quarterly* 21 (December 1967): 3.

Newspapers:

Daily Appeal (Carson City, Nev.): July 29, 1866.

Daily Index (Carson City, Nev.): March 24, 1886.

Daily Miner (Prescott, Ariz.): March 28, 1879.

Daily Reese River Reveille (Nev.): May 18–19, 1866; May 24, 1866.

CHAPTER 5
THE INNOCENTS

Meier, Gary & Gloria. *Oregon Outlaws.* Boise, Idaho: Tamarack Books, 1996.

Secrest, William B. *Perilous Trails, Dangerous Men.* Clovis, Calif.: Quill Driver Books, 2001.

Newspapers:

The Daily Oregonian (Portland, Ore.): July 16, 1872; July 22–23, 1872; July 25, 1872; July 27, 1872; August 21–24, 1872; August 26, 1872; February 7, 1876.

Idaho Statesman (Boise, Idaho): November 16, 1872; February 8, 1876; February 10, 1876.

CHAPTER 6
THE BOISE BANDITS

Newspapers:

Idaho Statesman (Boise, Idaho): November 11, 1875; November 16, 1875; February 3–5, 1876;

February 8, 1876; February 10, 1876; April 20, 1876; April 24–25, 1876; April 29, 1876; May 13, 1876; May 18, 1876; June 2, 1876; December 16, 1876.

CHAPTER 7
THE SHOWDOWN

Wilson, R. Michael. *Crime & Punishment in Early Arizona.* Las Vegas: Rama Press, 2004.

Newspapers:

Daily Citizen (Tucson, Ariz.): May 26, 1877; April 2, 1882.

Daily Miner (Prescott, Ariz.): February 19, 1875; March 15, 1875; May 18, 1877; May 25, 1877; April 26, 1878; May 10, 1878; September 19, 1878.

Arizona Enterprise (Prescott, Ariz.): May 4, 1878.

Arizona Sentinel (Yuma, Ariz.): May 19, 1877; May 26, 1877; June 9, 1877; July 7, 1877; November 30, 1877; December 7, 1877; August 19, 1882; August 26, 1882; October 14, 1882.

CHAPTER 8
THE MAN WHO SWALLOWED A WAGON WHEEL

Faber, Walter I. Personal interview with the author, May 14, 2001.

Hogan, William F. "John Miller: Pioneer Lawman." *Arizoniana* Vol. IV, no. 2 (Summer 1963).

Reeve, Frank D. "Albert Franklin Banta: Arizona Pioneer." Historical Society of New Mexico. *Publications in History* (September 1953).

Thrapp, Dan L. *Encyclopedia of Frontier Biography* (three volumes). Lincoln: University of Nebraska Press, 1988.

Walters, L. D. "How Bill Brazelton Was Killed." *Frontier Times,* August 1927, 24.

Wilson, R. Michael. "Brazen Bill Brazelton." *Wild West,* April 24, 2002.

Newspapers:

Arizona Enterprise (Prescott, Ariz.): August 21, 1878.

Arizona Sentinel (Yuma, Ariz.): May 19, 1878; August 10, 1878; August 17, 1878; August 24, 1878.

Daily Citizen (Tucson, Ariz.): May 5, 1877; October 6, 1877; August 2, 1878; August 8, 1878; August 16, 1878; August 23, 1878.

Daily Miner (Prescott, Ariz.): June 4, 1878; August 20–21, 1878; August 30, 1878.

Salt River Herald (Phoenix, Ariz.): August 3, 1878.

San Jose Evening News (Calif.): September 29, 1898.

CHAPTER 9
THE IRONCLAD STAGECOACH

Brown, Mabel E. "Robbery at Canyon Springs." *Bits and Pieces* Vol. 1, no. 2 (May 1965) p. 2.

McClintock, John S. *Pioneer Days in the Black Hills.* Norman: University of Oklahoma Press, 2000.

Randall, Arthur G. "Early Exploration of the Black Hills Area, Wyoming–South Dakota." *Wyoming Geological Association Guidebook.* (1988) p. 17.

Spring, Agnes W. *The Cheyenne and Black Hills Stage and Express Routes.* Lincoln: University of Nebraska Press, 1948.

Newspapers:

Cheyenne Daily Leader (Wyo.): September 25–26, 1878; September 28–29, 1878; October 1–6, 1878; October 10–11, 1878; October 17–18, 1878; October 25–26, 1878; November 5, 1878.

CHAPTER 10
A SHARP NEVADA ROAD AGENT

Block, Eugene B. *Great Stagecoach Robbers of the West.* Garden City, N.Y.: Doubleday & Company, 1962.

Secrest, William B. *Perilous Trails, Dangerous Men.* Clovis, Calif.: Quill Driver Books, 2001.

Newspapers:

Carson Daily Appeal (Nev.): June 8, 1880; June 15–17, 1880; June 22, 1880; September 5, 1880; September 9, 1880; September 11, 1880; September 14, 1880.

Territorial Enterprise (Virginia City, Nev.): May 16, 1880; June 15, 1880; August 10, 1880; September 7, 1880; September 14–15, 1880; September 19, 1880; September 21, 1880; September 23, 1880; October 1, 1880; October 7, 1880; October 12, 1880; November 2, 1880.

CHAPTER 11
A TEXAS BAD MAN IN COLORADO

Dugan, Mark. *Knight of the Road: The Life of Highwayman Ham White*. Athens: Ohio University Press, 1990.

Frye, Elnora L. *Atlas of Wyoming Outlaws at the Territorial Penitentiary*. Cheyenne: Wyoming Territorial Prison Corp., 1997.

Newspapers:

The Dailey News (Colo.): July 1–2, 1881; July 9, 1881; July 31, 1881; October 1, 1881.

CHAPTER 12
A LYNCHIN' BEE

Wilson, R. Michael. *Encyclopedia of Stagecoach Robbery in Arizona*. Las Vegas, Nev.: Rama Press, 2003.

Wilson, R. Michael. *Crime & Punishment in Early Arizona*. Las Vegas, Nev.: Rama Press, 2004.

Newspapers:

Arizona Enterprise (Florence, Ariz.): August 18, 1883; September 8, 1883; October 6, 1883.

Arizona Gazette (Phoenix, Ariz.): August 16, 1883; August 23, 1883; August 30, 1883;

September 3, 1883; September 6, 1883; September 13, 1883; September 15, 1883; October 4, 1883; November 22, 1883; August 2, 1884.

Weekly Citizen (Tuscon, Ariz.): August 1, 1883; August 18, 1883; September 8, 1883; September 15, 1883; September 29, 1883; October 5, 1883; October 13, 1883; November 1, 1884.

CHAPTER 13
ROBBERY AT SPEARFISH

Engebretson, Doug. "The Spearfish Mail Stage Hold-up." *True West,*
August 1987, 52.

Records of the United States Post Office Department. Case Files of
Investigations no. 61 (George Hayes) and no. 62 (Ulysses S.
Pitts): Records Group 28, Box 122–11E4/02/10/05.

Newspapers:

Argus Leader (Sioux Falls, S.D.): August 26, 1895; August 28–31, 1895.

Queen City Mail (Spearfish, S.D.): February 21, 1894; August 21, 1895;
September 4, 1895.

CHAPTER 14
ARIZONA'S PETTICOAT BANDIT

"An Arizona Episode," *Cosmopolitan* 27 (October 1899).

Block, Eugene B. *Great Stagecoach Robbers of the West.* Garden City,
N.Y.: Doubleday & Company, 1962.

Horan, David J. *Desperate Women.* New York: Bonanza Books, 1972.

McLoughlin, Denis. *Wild and Woolly, Encyclopedia of the Old West.* New
York: Barnes & Noble Books, 1975.

Wilson, R. Michael. *Encyclopedia of Stagecoach Robbery in Arizona.* Las
Vegas, Nev.: Rama Press, 2003.

Arizona. Las Vegas: RaMA PRESS, 2003.

Newspapers:

Arizona Graphic (Phoenix, Ariz.): January 27, 1900.

Arizona Republican (Phoenix, Ariz.): November 25, 1899; December 25,
1902.

Arizona Sentinel (Yuma, Ariz.): November 25, 1899; June 6, 1900;
December 17–18, 1902.

Arizona Star (Tucson, Ariz.): October 20, 1899; September 22, 1974.

Daily Citizen (Tucson, Ariz.): October 8, 1900; December 15, 1902.

Phoenix Sun (Ariz.): November 24, 1899.

CHAPTER 15
GOLD AT THE END OF THE RAINBOW

Freeman, Olga. "The Bungled Holdup of the Durkee Stage." *Real West,*
June 1971, 15.

Lee, Mabel B. *The Rainbow Years, A Happy Interlude.* Garden City, N.Y.:
Doubleday & Company, 1966.

Newspapers:

The Oregonian (Portland): April 6–7, 1915; April 9, 1915; June 26, 1915;
June 27, 1915.

CHAPTER 16
THE LAST STAGECOACH ROBBERY IN THE WEST

Bristow, Allen. "The Last Stagecoach Robbery." *True West*, January
1996, 28.

Penrose, Matt R. *Pots O' Gold.* Reno, Nev: A. Carlisle & Co., 1935.

Newspapers:

Carson Daily Appeal (Nev.): December 8, 1916; October 10, 1917;
October 20, 1917; March 2, 1918; April 16, 1918; September 5–6,
1918; December 10, 1918; December 14, 1918.

Elko Independent (Nev.): December 6, 1916; December 8, 1916;
December 12–15, 1916; September 18, 1917; September 22, 1917;
September 29, 1917; October 4–5, 1917; October 8, 1917.

INDEX

ABOUT THE AUTHOR

R. Michael Wilson has been researching the Old West for fifteen years, following a quarter century as a law enforcement officer in Southern California. He holds an Associate Degree in Police Science, a Bachelor's Degree in Criminology, a Master's Degree in Public Administration, and a Juris Doctorate degree.

R. Michael is an active member of the National Outlaw Lawman Association (NOLA) and Western Writers of America (WWA). He has five history books to his credit, all in his area of interest and expertise—crime and punishment in America's early West. His works represent his writing philosophy: "The truth, the whole truth, and nothing but the truth."